Progress in IS

More information about this series at http://www.springer.com/series/10440

Anders Hjalmarsson · Gustaf Juell-Skielse
Paul Johannesson

Open Digital Innovation

A Contest Driven Approach

Anders Hjalmarsson
University of Borås & RISE Viktoria
Gothenburg
Sweden

Paul Johannesson
Stockholm University
Stockholm
Sweden

Gustaf Juell-Skielse
Stockholm University & RISE Viktoria
Stockholm
Sweden

ISSN 2196-8705
Progress in IS
ISBN 978-3-319-85889-0
DOI 10.1007/978-3-319-56339-8

ISSN 2196-8713 (electronic)

ISBN 978-3-319-56339-8 (eBook)

Printed on acid-free paper

This Springer imprint is published by Springer Nature
The registered company is Springer International Publishing AG
The registered company address is: Gewerbestrasse 11, 6330 Cham, Switzerland

Preface

This book came about to support the practice of contests to manage innovation and to provide a state-of-the art survey for conducting research in open digital innovation contests. Contests combine creativity and business with fun and have become popular means for stimulating the development of services for the digitalization of society.

Through its activity descriptions and guidelines, this book provides a practically useful approach to innovation for managers and policy makers. It helps contest organizers to build the momentum to engage in open data innovation, and it offers a set of strategies for managing innovation barriers. Also, it can serve as a textbook on graduate and undergraduate courses in digital innovation and entrepreneurship.

The content of the book is based on longitudinal action design research that we have conducted over the past five years. It involves multiple digital innovation contests in Europe, Asia and Latin America and has given us access to a rich data set on open innovation. During our research journey, we have been able to support the contest organizers with theoretically anchored advice while at the same time create and field-test the approach presented in the book.

Our thanks to Daniel Rudmark for his contributions in the area of third-party development. Results that have become an integral part of Chaps. 6 and 9. Our thanks also to Workneh Ayele whose work on innovation measurement forms the foundation of Chap. 15 and to Elea Juell-Skielse who developed the initial framework of strategic options presented in Chap. 12. Finally, we want to express our gratitude to Sweden's innovation agency Vinnova for providing the necessary research grants.

Gothenburg, Sweden   Anders Hjalmarsson
Stockholm, Sweden   Gustaf Juell-Skielse
Stockholm, Sweden   Paul Johannesson

Contents

Chapter 1
Introduction

Abstract This chapter provides a background to the book. It introduces the notion of innovation and discusses how it can be managed, in particular through innovation contests. A life-cycle perspective on innovation contests is introduced, which shows how a contest moves through the phases of pre-contest, contest, and post-contest. This perspective is used throughout the book and the activities of the life-cycle are described and analysed in separate chapters, moving from goal setting and stakeholder engagement over operations management to business model design and barrier management.

1.1 Introduction

Innovation is about coming up with new ideas, developing new products and processes, and implementing new solutions in the social and economic life of people. A common view is that innovation is spontaneous, emergent and unpredictable. It is a largely creative endeavour that is notoriously difficult to manage as discussed by Fagerberg et al. (2006). However, Terwiesch and Ulrich (2009) argue that innovation can be successfully managed, and this can be done by focusing on opportunities. The key goal of innovation management is to generate many new ideas, filter out the best ones, and then refine them into opportunities.

An increasingly popular approach for managing innovation is the open innovation contest, which is about an organisation inviting participants and offering them a prize for submitting new ideas and solutions. Some examples of open innovation contests are Travelhack, the Open Stockholm Award, the Volvo Car Challenge, the Electricity Innovation Challenge and the Olympic City Transport Challenge, five contests organised in Scandinavia as well as in Brazil in both single and recurrent events between 2011 and 2016. These and other contests, used as running examples in this book, are introduced in Chap. 3.

Innovation contests add an element of competition to the innovation process by letting several participants challenge each other to come up with the best contributions. And, more importantly, open innovation contests constitute an open

A. Hjalmarsson et al., *Open Digital Innovation*, Progress in IS,
DOI 10.1007/978-3-319-56339-8_1

process, in which an organisation enables people outside it to contribute to its innovation.

Open innovation contests can take place in any industrial and societal context, but recently many organisations have initiated open digital innovation contests. These are contests in which the organiser makes various digital resources available to the contest participants who can use them to build novel digital services; e.g. Resledaren "a smartphone based digital service that enables people with cognitive dysfunction to use public transport", PAW—ProActive Wipers "an integrated digital service that provides enhanced driver support in future cars", and RioGo "a smartphone based service that provides personalised advice on how to travel to different events during the Olympics based on your own event schedule".

Though open digital innovation contests offer great promise and there are many examples of highly successful contests, it is still challenging to organise such contests in a way that fully realise their potential. Contest organisers need principles and guidelines for designing and managing contests as well as benefitting from their outcomes. The goal of this book is to offer such principles and guidelines in an easily accessible format. The book takes a life cycle perspective, emphasising how open digital innovation moves through the phases of pre-contest, contest and post-contest. See Fig. 1.1.

Within the phases, there are a number of activities carried out iteratively:

- Pre-contest phase—this phase consists of the activities before the contest starts. Its main activities are: *set goals*, in which the goals of the contest are established; *engage stakeholders*, in which contest participants, resource providers and potential beneficiaries are identified and attracted; *design contest*, in which the contest is designed and planned; and *develop platform*, in which a platform for the contest's digital resources is created.
- Contest phase—this phase consists of the activities carried out during the contest. Its main activities are: *motivate developers*, in which developers are motivated to participate in the contest; *manage operations*, in which the contest is managed on a day-to-day basis and *evaluate contributions*, in which the contest contributions are evaluated and the winners are selected.

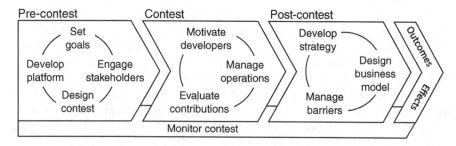

Fig. 1.1 A life-cycle perspective on open digital innovation contests

- Post-contest phase—this phase consists of the activities carried out after the contest. Its main activities are: *develop strategy*, in which a strategy for the relationship between the contest organiser and participants is established; *design business model*, in which a business model for exploiting the contest contributions is created; *manage barriers*, in which barriers for exploiting the contributions are identified and addressed.

The book is primarily intended for managers and policy makers of open digital innovation who are interested in contests in order to stimulate the innovation process. It can also serve as a text on graduate and undergraduate courses in digital innovation and entrepreneurship. The book does not only offer an analysis of key issues in open digital innovation contests but also provides tools for improving the contests, including motivation factors, digital support platforms, a measurement model for evaluating open digital innovation and instruments for overcoming innovation barriers.

Chapter 2 offers an introduction to open innovation and digital innovation, while Chap. 3 discusses how contests can be used for stimulating open digital innovation. These chapters can be skipped by the reader who is already familiar with these notions. Chapter 4 provides an overview of the suggested approach for preparing, managing and benefitting from the contests. The approach is divided into the three phases of pre-contest, contest and post-contest, and each includes a set of activities. See Fig. 1.1. In total, there are eleven activities, each of which is described in a chapter of its own, making up the main part of the book from Chaps. 5–11. It is recommended to start with Chap. 4 in order to get an overall understanding of the approach, and it is then possible to read the remaining chapters in any order as they are essentially self-contained.

References

Fagerberg, J., Mowery, D. C., & Nelson, R. R. (2006). *The Oxford handbook of innovation*. Oxford: Oxford University Press.
Terwiesch, C., & Ulrich, K. T. (2009). *Innovation tournaments: Creating and selecting exceptional opportunities*. Brighton: Harvard Business Press.

Chapter 2
Open Innovation

Abstract This chapter introduces the notion of open innovation, which is about organizations making use of external ideas, solutions and technologies instead of only relying on its internal innovation. Three different forms of open innovation are discussed: inside-out, outside-in and coupled innovation, which differ with regard to the direction of the idea flows. The chapter also introduces a number of models for open innovation, including crowdsourcing, product platforming, collaborative innovation networks, and innovation contests. Digital innovation has transformed many businesses, enabling new kinds of smart, connected products as well as novel business models based on platforms.

Innovation is about new ideas, new products, or new processes. Innovation can be radical such as the digital computer, or it can be incremental such as new batteries with longer lifetimes. Sometimes, innovation is taken in a broader sense and is seen as the result of processes that combine novel ideas and products, with an impact on society at large.

Innovation can take place anywhere in society: in universities, in companies, at governments, among individuals, etc. It has often been the case that the innovations needed by an organisation have been produced by that organisation itself. In fact, there has sometimes even been resistance to using innovations generated elsewhere, as evidenced by the "not invented here" syndrome. This kind of innovation that takes place entirely within an organisation is commonly called *closed innovation*. While closed innovation can be successful for an organisation, it suffers from one major limitation: most of the smart and innovative people in any area work outside that organisation.

As a response to the limitations of closed innovation, the notion of *open innovation* has been proposed, defined by Chesbrough (2006) as "a paradigm that assumes that firms can and should use external ideas, as well as internal ideas and internal and external paths to market, as the firms look to advance their technology" (p. xxiv). Organisations should not only rely on their own resources for innovation but also make use of external ideas, technologies and people. Complementarily, organisations should also open up their own innovation so it can benefit others.

A. Hjalmarsson et al., *Open Digital Innovation*, Progress in IS,
DOI 10.1007/978-3-319-56339-8_2

There are three forms of openness in open innovation, outside-in, inside-out and coupled. In the *outside-in* form, the initiator of open innovation unlocks its organisational borders to make use of external ideas and technologies. In the *inside-out* form, openness refers to situations in which the initiator of open innovation unlocks its own resources so that external people, e.g. developers, can use them. In this way, unused innovations are made accessible to others. Outside-in and inside-out open innovation can also be combined into a *coupled process* in which organisations work in alliances that involve both giving and taking.

Open innovation puts new demands on organisations' competence, so-called absorptive and desorptive capacity (Lichtenthaler and Lichtenthaler 2009). Absorptive capacity is the ability that an organisation has to evaluate and use external knowledge related to the outside-in form of openness. Desorptive capacity is an organisation's ability to exploit internal knowledge through external people, relating to the inside-out form of openness.

2.1 Models for Open Innovation

Open innovation can take many different forms, including crowdsourcing, product platforming, collaborative innovation networks and innovation contests.

2.1.1 Crowdsourcing

As defined by Merriam-Webster, crowdsourcing is "the practice of obtaining needed services, ideas, or content by soliciting contributions from a large group of people and especially from the online community rather than from traditional employees or suppliers". The word is a combination of "crowd" and "outsourcing" and the idea is to outsource work to a crowd. For innovation, the crowd could consist of customers of the outsourcing organisation but it could comprise external developers or suppliers and partners. Crowdsourcing is not a new phenomenon, for example, in 1714 the British government offered the public a monetary prize to whoever could provide the best solution to determining the longitude of a ship at sea. But crowdsourcing has become increasingly popular in recent years thanks to the opportunities offered by online platforms.

2.1.2 Product Platforming

A *product platform* consists of a tool kit and other resources that contributors can exploit, modify and extend. Examples of such platforms are mobile operating systems, which developers can use to build and distribute their mobile apps. Other examples are SDKs (Software Development Kits), such as the Eclipse platform, which provide environments for designing software. Product platforms offer a common basis around which an organisation and external contributors can work together and generate innovations. As platforms typically are long-lasting, they provide opportunities for continuing and deeply integrated cooperation.

2.1.3 Collaborative Innovation Network

As defined by Gloor (2006), a *collaborative innovation network* is "a cyber-team of self-motivated people with a collective vision, enabled by the Web to collaborate in achieving a common goal by sharing ideas, information and work" (p. 4). Members of such a network collaborate and communicate directly with each other, instead of using hierarchies. They are intrinsically motivated and work together in order to support a cause or advance an idea. By participating in innovation networks, an organisation can both obtain ideas and innovations from the network and share its own ones. Thus, innovation networks enable outside-in as well as inside-out and coupled open innovation.

2.1.4 Innovation Contest

An *innovation contest* is an event in which an organiser invites participants and offers a prize for submitting innovations in the forms of ideas, prototypes, products or services. Chapter 3 (and the entire book) is dedicated to digital innovation contests.

2.2 Digital Innovation

Thanks to recent technical developments, novel ICT (Information and Communication Technology) solutions have been applied in many new areas. Social media technology has enabled social platforms, such as Facebook, LinkedIn and Twitter. Mobile technology has resulted in new communication devices, including smartphones and tablets. The Internet of Things has made it possible to combine digital solutions with well-established products resulting in enhanced or novel products, e.g. robot vacuum cleaners and self-driving cars.

This kind of digital innovation does not only apply to products and services but also to processes and business models. An example is Airbnb that uses a digital solution for matching travellers with people who have a room to rent. Another example is Uber that allows almost any car owner to become a taxi driver and lets customers find and order taxis using their smartphones. The innovation of these companies does not reside in the services they offer but in their business models, i.e. how they connect actors in a network to create value.

Open data have recently become a key resource for digital innovation. The idea behind open data is that data should be free for everyone to use, reuse and distribute. There should not exist any restrictions in the form of copyrights, licenses, patents or other control mechanisms. As stated by the Open Definition (http://opendefinition.org/) "Open means anyone can freely access, use, modify and share for any purpose (subject, at most, to requirements that preserve provenance and openness)." Open government data have been advocated as a means for strengthening democracy as well as economic growth through digital innovation. By making government information accessible as open data distributed via APIs, novel services can be designed that improve transparency, accountability and public participation in decision processes. Open government data can also create business opportunities by enabling companies to develop services that process, integrate, distribute and present the data in new ways.

Open data can be used in many ways for open innovation. An example of inside-out openness is an organisation that provides open data through APIs to external developers. A digital service generated from this form of distributed development could either become viable outside the data providing organisation, or become a part of the digital service repertoire within the organisation. The latter scenario is an example of a coupled innovation process, meaning that the development initiative gradually moves back inside the data provider again, after external knowledge has been used to speed up the innovation process.

2.3   Read More

A classic text on open innovation is the book by Chesbrough (2006), which contrasts closed and open innovation, investigates business models for open innovation as well as the management of intellectual property and presents a number of case studies from large corporations. The Open Innovation Community offers a web site that "serves as an informational resource for thought leaders, consultants, authors, business leaders, academics and others who have a deep interest in open innovation" (http://openinnovation.net/).

Gassmann and Enkel (2004) introduce three process archetypes for open innovation: the outside-in process, the inside-out process and the coupled process. They suggest that the future of innovation is not about outsourcing internal innovation, but about following a flexible innovation strategy that includes outsourcing ventures, reintegrating new businesses, scanning and integrating new technologies and connecting external sources to the internal innovation process. Surowiecki (2005) investigates a key insight behind crowdsourcing: large groups of people can be smarter than an elite few and better at solving problems, fostering innovation and coming to wise decisions.

Lichtentaler and Lichtentaler discuss competences related to open innovation. In their framework they distinguish between internal and external competences and a firm's capacity to explore knowledge from other firms as well as their capacity to exploit knowledge through inside-out type of innovation processes.

References

Chesbrough, H. W. (2006). *Open innovation: The new imperative for creating and profiting from technology*. Brighton: Harvard Business Press.

Gassmann, O., & Enkel, E. (2004). Towards a theory of open innovation: Three core process archetypes. In *R&D Management Conference* (Vol. 6).

Gloor, P. A. (2006). *Swarm creativity: Competitive advantage through collaborative innovation networks*. Oxford: Oxford University Press.

http://opendefinition.org/

http://openinnovation.net/

Lichtenthaler, U., & Lichtenthaler, E. (2009). A capability-based framework for open innovation: Complementing absorptive capacity. *Journal of Management Studies, 46*(8), 1315–1338.

Surowiecki, J. (2005). *The wisdom of crowds*. Anchor.

Chapter 3
Open Digital Innovation Contest

Abstract This chapter introduces open digital innovation contests that aim to develop digital services. Key stakeholders in such contests are identified: organisers, participants, resource providers, and beneficiaries. A classification of digital innovation contests is proposed based on the length of a contest and its inclusiveness. Other design elements of contests are also discussed, including media, target group and evaluation. It is argued that innovation contests can be viewed as innovation intermediaries that help to connect actors in an innovation system. Advantages and disadvantages of innovation contests are discussed. Finally, six contests are introduced, which serve as running examples throughout the book.

Open digital innovation contests are competitions that aim to develop digital services. Based on the work by Hjalmarsson and Rudmark (2012), they can be described as events in which external developers compete to design and implement innovative and solid digital service prototypes, based on digital resources made available by the organiser. There are three key ingredients in this definition. First, the participants of the contests are to be external developers, i.e. developers outside the organisation that arranges the competition. In this way, new categories of people are drawn into the innovation system around an organisation, thereby enabling open innovation. Furthermore, the goal is to develop a digital service prototype; it is not sufficient just to suggest a new idea or create a product without digital content. Finally, the service developed is to be based on digital resources made available by the organiser.

3.1 Stakeholders in Digital Innovation Contests

A digital innovation contest is a highly social undertaking involving different kinds of stakeholders. First, there is the *organiser* who sets up and runs the contest. It also makes digital resources available to the external developers. Sometimes, the organiser can be a single organisation, but it is common that several organisations

A. Hjalmarsson et al., *Open Digital Innovation*, Progress in IS,
DOI 10.1007/978-3-319-56339-8_3

with complementary competencies form a team and organise the contest together. Second, there are the *participants* in the contest, who are external developers who take part in the contest and create service prototypes. Participants can be both individuals and teams and they can have different backgrounds, such as being citizens, students, entrepreneurs or professional developers. Third, there are the *resource providers*, who offer digital resources as well as other building blocks to be used by the participants. A resource provider can offer data, digital services and support tools, but also financial means and know-how. Fourth, there are the *beneficiaries* who benefit from the results of the contest. Clearly, the organiser is always a beneficiary as are the participants and the resource providers. But, also, potential users of solutions based on the prototypes generated can be beneficiaries as well as innovation communities and society at large.

3.2   Kinds of Innovation Contests

Digital innovation contests are to generate digital service prototypes and they, therefore, constitute a special case of contests and competitions in open innovation. In general, such contests aim to produce any kind of product or service or even just an idea or a design sketch. Many different words and phrases are used for talking about innovation contests, e.g. innovation competition, innovation tournament, idea jam, design contest and design prize. These words do not have a fixed meaning and different people use them in different ways. But they indicate important differences between innovation contests that have to do with purpose, time and the degree of inclusiveness.

Innovation contests are used for many purposes. From the organiser's perspective, they can help to generate more ideas that can be transformed into products and services. They can help to select from among competing ideas and filter out those that are the most promising. They can also help to improve the visibility and image of the organiser by creating a buzz and drawing attention to the organiser and its brands. Yet another purpose is to strengthen the size and dynamism of an innovation community in which the organiser participates. For open digital innovation contests, a related purpose is to investigate the opportunities that an open data platform can offer an innovation community. Feedback from an innovation contest can then help the organiser to understand which of the data offered is seen as most useful by the developers, what additional data could be valuable, and which delivery channels are most appropriate.

The time period of an innovation contest can vary. Some contests are very short and intensive, maybe only a few days during which developers meet, create and present their contributions and get them evaluated. But innovation contests can also go on during an extended period of time, weeks or months, during which developers produce their ideas, designs and prototypes. Such long running contests may also include multiple rounds of evaluations, similar to large sporting events. This means that weak contributions can be filtered out at an early stage, while stronger ideas can be developed and evaluated more carefully.

Innovation contests can be more or less inclusive with respect to participation. The most open form would accept anyone entering the contest. A closed form would only include invited participants. Then there are all the forms in between, for example, restricting participation to certain kinds of people (individuals, companies, public sector organisations, etc.) or people with specific qualifications (educational degree, competence in an industry, etc.). Four types of innovation contests can be distinguished by combining the dimensions of the time period and the degree of inclusiveness, see Fig. 3.1. An innovation jam is only for a short time and very inclusive; it is useful for generating many new ideas. An innovation cup is also inclusive but the time is extended; it is helpful for strengthening an innovation community. An innovation battle is short and exclusive; it can be used for quickly identifying strong opportunities for novel digital services based on the open digital resources available at the contest. An innovation challenge is long and exclusive; it can help an organiser to decide whether to build or procure. Consequently, the innovation challenge may be used as part of a procurement process or as an initiator to a development process with the objective of creating a new digital service to be launched on an end-user market.

The key notions introduced so far are summarised in Fig. 3.2, showing the four types of stakeholders as well as the four types of open digital innovation contests. The figure also indicates that resource providers provide digital resources that are used by participants to produce service prototypes, which can benefit beneficiaries.

	Inclusive recruitment	Exclusive recruitment	
Short contest	"Innovation Jam" *Promote and stimulate*	"Innovation Battle" *What is possible?*	Short contest
Long contest	"Innovation Cup" *Strengthen and catalyze*	"Innovation Challenge" *What should we buy or build?*	Long contest
	Inclusive recruitment	Exclusive recruitment	

Fig. 3.1 Types of innovation contests

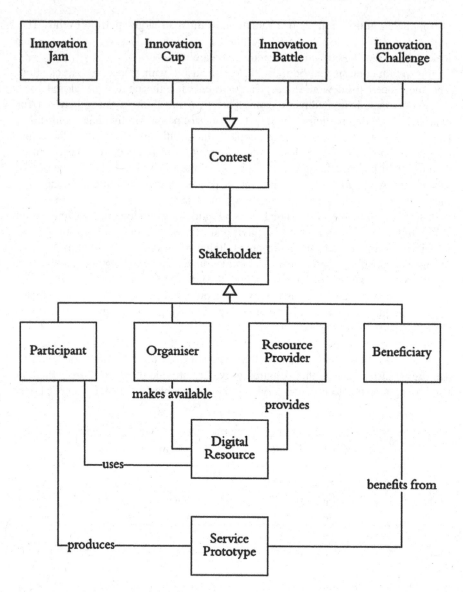

Fig. 3.2 Key notions of open digital innovation contests

3.3 Innovation Contests as Innovation Intermediaries

In open innovation, different kinds of agents act and interact to create, adopt and diffuse innovations. Together, they constitute an innovation system. The components of an innovation system include participants, who can be public or private organisations as well as institutions, i.e., rules, laws, habits and practices that govern and regulate the interactions and relationships between the participants. Typical interactions in an innovation system are business transactions but also learning processes, in which knowledge is exchanged between organisations not necessarily managed as business transactions.

The key participants of an innovation system of open data services are open data suppliers, developers and end users. But innovation systems often include participants who fulfil bridging and brokerage roles, so called innovation intermediaries. These intermediaries do not innovate or use innovations themselves but, instead, help other participants to do so. They help to connect potential providers, facilitate business transactions, help to find advice and funding support and, in general, act as mediators. This helps to overcome constraints in an innovation system.

By organising digital innovation contests, participants in an innovation system try to motivate others, both to engage in open service innovation and to transfer information between each other about available open data and available solutions. Hence, organisers of digital innovation contests take on the role of innovation intermediaries, stimulating the development of new open services.

3.3.1 Design Elements of Open Digital Innovation Contests

Setting up a digital innovation contest can be seen as a design process, in which the organiser identifies and configures a number of design elements. The list of design elements is open ended and some of them can be unique to a particular contest, but there are a number of key elements that appear in every contest:

- *Media.* Innovation contests can make use of different kinds of media and they can be offline, online or mixed.
- *Organiser.* The organiser can be a company, a public organisation, an industry consortium, an NGO or even an individual.
- *Task/topic specificity.* The topic of the contest and the task to be carried out by the contestants can be more or less well-specified; sometimes they are very open, leaving room for the participants to explore many ideas, while, sometimes, they are very specific.
- *Degree of elaboration.* Some contests only require ideas as contributions, while others may require design sketches, prototypes or even fully functioning solutions.
- *Target group.* The most open innovation contests will accept anyone as a participant, while others may restrict participation, e.g. to companies in a certain industry or to individuals with specific qualifications.
- *Eligibility.* Eligibility determines who is allowed to participate: individuals, teams or both.

- *Contest period.* Contest periods can be very short (some hours to a maximum of 14 days), short (15 days to 6 weeks), long (6 weeks to 4 months) or very long (more than four months/indefinite).
- *Reward/motivation.* Motivation can be built by intrinsic as well as extrinsic motivators. Extrinsic motivators include awards and prizes, while intrinsic motivators include fun, reputation and self-realisation.
- *Community functionality.* Community functionality is provided by applications that support interaction, information exchange, community building and collaborative product design, e.g. through social media, web sites and tailor-made development platforms.
- *Evaluation.* The evaluation of contributions can be carried out by different people, resulting in self-assessment, peer review or evaluation by a jury of experts.

3.3.2 Pitfalls in Organising Innovation Contests

Organisers of open digital innovation contests encounter many kinds of pitfalls both before, during and after the contest:

Pre-contest

- *Unclear goals.* The organiser does not make the goals of the contest clear. There can be different goals for a contest, such as filtering out solutions or improving the organiser's brand, and it is perfectly fine to combine several goals. But they should be made clear and explicit.
- *Fragmented audience.* The organiser targets a too fragmented audience. Depending on the contest goals, it is often required to focus on a specific group of potential participants, for example suppliers, customers or university students. However, there are also cases where it is appropriate to invite anyone to the contest independently of his or her background.
- *Too broad or too narrow tasks.* The organiser does not define the contest tasks with an appropriate specificity. The tasks should be so broad that they are understandable and interesting for a large audience but also so narrow that the contributions result in relevant and useful solutions.

Contest

- *Too few resources allocated.* The organiser allocates too few resources for interacting with the contest participants. The participants may need a lot of support and ask for a great deal of interaction during the contest, and the organiser needs to be able to handle these requests.
- *Changing the rules.* The organiser changes the rules during the contest. In order to keep the trust and commitments of the participants, the organiser should stick to the rules that have been announced including those for deadlines and awards.

Post-contest

- *Insufficient support to participants.* The organiser does not support the participants in further developing their solution after the contest. If a goal is to
transform the prototype delivered by a participant into a working service, many
resources are required. Therefore, the organiser may need to support the participant with financial resources, market knowledge, technology resources
and/or other kinds of resources.

3.4   Advantages and Disadvantages of Digital Innovation Contests

Innovation contests can offer important advantages for their organisers. By
involving external developers, the results of a contest can help to reduce the cost of
research and development for the organiser. External developers can also provide
fresh and original ideas that would not have been developed within the organisation, thereby increasing the chances for radical innovation. Additionally, there is a
potential for synergy between internal and external developers. This synergy can be
particularly valuable for an organiser with limited digital experience and competence, as a digital innovation contest can bring in developers with complementary
competences. Another kind of advantage is that an innovation contest can
strengthen the status or brand of the organiser, by providing visibility and pro-
jecting an image of openness and innovation. The format of an open contest also
enables viral marketing, as the word spreads among developers who could be
interested in participating in the contest.

There are, however, also potential risks and disadvantages with a digital innovation contest. One is that the organiser incidentally reveals information that is not
intended for sharing. This could, in some cases, even result in losing a competitive
advantage due to revealing intellectual property. More generally, the organiser can
lose control by inviting external developers into its own innovation processes.
However, compared to other forms of open innovation, an innovation contest offers
the organiser the means to regulate and incorporate external innovation. The
remaining chapters of the book will show how this can be done in a systematic
manner.

3.5   Cases as Running Examples in the Book

In the book, eleven contests are used as running examples to illustrate different
aspects when organising an open digital innovation. The contests were held in
Scandinavia and Brazil between 2011 and 2016. The authors have acted as either

organisers or evaluators in these cases and have, therefore, access to rich data material from each event.

- *Westcoast Travelhack 2011*. With the aim of attracting external developers to a new portal with APIs to open public transport data in Sweden (Trafiklab.se), Travelhack 2011 was organised in October 2011 in Gothenburg, Sweden. The contest format was a 24-hour innovation jam and yielded twenty digital, mostly smartphone based, apps with the joint aim of boosting sustainable personal transport.
- *Travelhack 2012 Oslo*. InformNorden, Norwegian National Railway (NSB) and Trafikanten organised a second Travelhack in 2012 located in Oslo main central train station. The contest format was a 24-hour innovation battle with four teams with professional external developers. The aim was to probe what would be the outcome if specific data sets, currently not released as open data, were made accessible to external developers.
- *Volvo Car Challenge 2013*. The theme for the Volvo Car Challenge was integrated safety and driver support. The format for the contest was a staged innovation challenge. Between March and June 2013, twelve invited teams competed to develop qualified ideas for digital prototypes that adhered to the contest theme. Three of the teams were rewarded funds to transform their ideas into operational prototypes and, amongst these three, one team was selected as the winner with the chance of a commercial contract with Volvo Cars.
- *Travelhack 2013 Sweden*. With the combined aims of: (1) attracting new developers to Trafiklab.se and: (2) generating innovative digital services which would strengthen the attractiveness of public transport, Samtrafiken, Storstockholms Lokaltrafik and Viktoria Swedish ICT organised the third instalment of Travelhack in Stockholm 2013. The contest format selected was the innovation cup format with an idea phase, a refinement phase and a finale in the form of a 24-hour hackathon. Over 200 interested teams signed up in the idea phase, generating fifty-four qualified submitted ideas. A screening of these ideas resulted in the selection of twenty-four teams who were invited to refine their own ideas during a one-month preparation phase. The finale was organised in mid-March 2013 as a 24-hour hackathon resulting in three different theme-winners and an overall winner of the competition.
- *Volvo Car Challenge UX 2014*. Following the same format as Volvo Car Challenge 2013, the second instalment of the contest was organised in 2013 with the theme user experience. In addition to influencing development of new value creating services, the aim was also to encourage development outside the hosting vehicle OEM, explore the capacity in technical platforms and explore what value could be created through the use of new development processes. The contest was organised in collaboration with the Vehicle ICT arena in Gothenburg, Sweden. The contest generated eighteen ideas by ten participating teams. Three teams were awarded funds to transform their ideas into working service prototypes and an overall winner was selected at the end of the contest.

- *Travelhack 2014 Norway.* The fourth instalment of Travelhack was organised in May 2014 by a consortium of ten organisations, including NSB, Viktoria Swedish ICT, Startup Norway, University of Oslo and Transportøkenomisk Institutt. The contest had two tracks. One professional track was organised as an innovation battle and one open track was organised as an innovation jam. Both tracks were 24 h events that were located at the national railway innovation centre in Drammen, Norway. Seventeen teams joined the open track and seven teams attended the professional track. The aim with the open track was to stimulate external developers to produce digital service prototypes that enhance the travelling experience when using public transport. In order to stimulate development, open data as well as traveller persona were provided to the developers. The aim with the professional track was to test a new form of public procurement. The teams who attended this track were challenged to develop a prototype for a widget that could be included in the tablet that would be the principal information device for train personnel in Norway.
- *Open Stockholm Award 2014.* The contest was organised as a two-month staged innovation challenge. It attracted participants from fourteen countries and generated ninety-three contributions based on open data sources provided by the City of Stockholm, Stockholm region and private enterprises. In order to support the contestants, four meetings were organised and communication was chan- nelled via a contest platform. Two winning teams shared the winner's prize. One of the winners had developed an app for optimising on- and off-load zones in the city, while the other team developed an app for citizens and visitors to help them find restaurants and pubs during the visit.
- *Goods Distribution Challenge 2014.* The City of Gothenburg, together with Viktoria Swedish ICT, the Swedish Transport Administration, DB Schenker, DHL, DSV and Renova organised the Goods Distribution Challenge in Gothenburg in the spring of 2014. The contest followed the innovation cup format and invited external developers to build digital services based on open data that would enhance road transport predictability in city areas. The specific open data used consisted of data sets related to disturbances in the road network, but the teams were, in addition, allowed to use supplementary data to make their services work. The threshold for participation in the contest was high, conse- quently only ten teams participated with four teams contributing with opera- tional prototypes. The winning team won support to submit applications for funding as well as support from the participating transport companies to test the prototype in a live setting.
- *Volvo Trucks Open Innovation Challenge 2015.* The purpose of the contest was to encourage external developers to build IT services that created benefits for the vehicle industry, using the platform Automotive Grade Android (AGA). The platform is an open development platform developed and operated by Vehicle ICT Arena and partners in Gothenburg, Sweden. Through the platform, external developers can use data sets and signals, e.g. GPS-positioning, speed and fuel consumption, to build novel digital services that could be implemented in current or next generation vehicles. The contest attracted both students,

start-up and professional teams, and was organised as a staged innovation challenge with a final hackathon.

- *Electricity Innovation Challenge 2015*. Electricity Innovation Challenge 2015 was an open innovation contest that took place in Gothenburg in Autumn 2015. The contest attracted forty-eight teams who developed suggestions for innovations aimed at making tomorrow's bus trips more attractive. The goal was to develop prototypes that could be exposed and tested live in ElectriCity after the challenge. Competing teams had, in addition to expert advice and methodological support, among other things, access to new open real-time data from the buses and drawings and plans for the bus stops. This was made available via the Electricity's innovation platform. Additionally, the challenge offered expert advice and methodological support throughout the contest in four development workshops.

- *Olympic City Transport Challenge 2015–2016*. This contest was organised in Rio de Janeiro prior to the Olympics in the city in 2016. The theme for Olympic City Transport Challenge was "How do we make Rio public transport and urban sustainable mobility more reliable, comfortable and accessible?" The contest was divided into three categories: Travel planner, Comfort and accessibility, and Experience the Olympics. The building blocks made available for external developers participating in the contest were transport data and user persona illustrating different challenges for personal transportation in the city. The challenge was a part of the protocol of intentions signed by Empresa Municipal de Informática—IplanRio, the Rio Operations Centre (Centro de Operações Rio) and Viktoria Swedish ICT, to design and manage a research process based on the mobility data available in the data.rio website—the City Hall's open data catalogue. Besides facilitating the mobility of the city before and after the Rio 2016 Games, the challenge became an opportunity to empower local and international external developers. Sixteen teams enrolled for the first phase of the challenge. The teams spanned individual developers and start-ups to medium and large companies, from seven different countries. Divided into the three categories—Comfort and Accessibility, Experience the Olympics and Travel Planner—nine projects reached the final prototype phase. The users of the winning services will benefit from the ease of information provided; e.g. better selection of routes when crossing the city, better combination of public transport resources, better bus stop indication for people with disabilities, and personalised information about Olympic events and other tourist/cultural activities throughout the city.

3.6   Further Reading

Terwiesch and Ulrich (2009) have written a book on innovation contests in which they focus on generating promising opportunities which are then evaluated and filtered in a contest. Thereby, it is possible to arrive at exceptional opportunities in a methodical and systematic way. The role of the organisers of contests as innovation intermediaries are discussed by Juell-Skielse et al. (2014). The design elements for open digital innovation contests are based on the work by Bullinger et al. (2010) and Hjalmarsson and Rudmark (2012). An overview of different kinds of contests is given by Adamczyk et al. (2012). Pitfalls are discussed in (http://www.100open. com/2016/01/10-dos-donts-for-open-innovation-competitions/).

References

Adamczyk, S., Bullinger, A. C., & Möslein, K. M. (2012). Innovation contests: A review, classification and outlook. *Creativity and Innovation Management, 21*(4), 335–360.

Bullinger, A. C., et al. (2010). Community-based innovation contests: Where competition meets cooperation. *Creativity and Innovation Management, 19*(3), 290–303.

Hjalmarsson, A., & Rudmark, D. (2012). Designing digital innovation contests. In *Design Science Research in Information Systems. Advances in Theory and Practice*. Berlin, Heidelberg: Springer.

Juell-Skielse, G., Hjalmarsson, A., Juell-Skielse, E., Johannesson, P., & Rudmark, D. (2014). Contests as innovation intermediaries in open data markets. *Information Polity, 19*(3, 4), 247–262.

Terwiesch, C., & Ulrich, K. T. (2009). *Innovation tournaments: Creating and selecting exceptional opportunities*. Harvard Business Press.

Chapter 4
Organising Open Digital Innovation Contests

Abstract This chapter introduces a structured approach to support organisers of open digital innovation contests. It supports organisers to design and operate contests to achieve intended outcomes and effects. First, the logic of the model is presented. Then each phase in the model is described and key activities are highlighted. The following chapters describe each activity in detail.

4.1 A Structured Approach

Figure 4.1 provides an illustration of the approach for how to design and operate open digital innovation contests from the idea to a viable digital service prototype. However, each open digital innovation contest has to be carefully organised for its specific goals using the approach as guidance.

The approach supports organisers' ambitions to involve external developers in the innovation of digital services based on digital resources made available to them. A contest will involve a number of stakeholders and the approach promotes shared understanding of the contest process. Moreover, organising innovation as a contest requires a focus at the nexus of innovation, performed by others while retaining control over the innovation process.

The key message of the model can be summarised as follows: Open digital innovation provides a complement to traditional models of digital service development by distributing the innovation practice to networks of developers external to the contest organisers. The success of open digital innovation requires an organisational form that both stimulates external developers to participate and supports the organisers to keep control over the innovation process and its outcomes.

The approach consists of three phases and includes eleven activities. It has a pedagogical function and should not be too strictly interpreted in terms of temporality. For example, goals are set early but can change over time, for instance, when a new stakeholder enters the organising team. Another example is that the

© Springer International Publishing AG 2017
A. Hjalmarsson et al., *Open Digital Innovation*, Progress in IS,
DOI 10.1007/978-3-319-56339-8_4

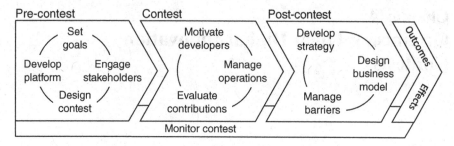

Fig. 4.1 Approach for organising open digital innovation contests

contest support platform, which is established prior to the contest, may be enhanced
when the contest is running due to new digital resources becoming available to the
contest participants.

4.2 The Pre-contest Phase

The pre-contest phase constitutes the starting point for the approach. It includes a
set of four interrelated activities that are performed to plan and prepare for the
contest: *Set goals, engage stakeholders, design contest and develop platform*. The
goals are the starting point for determining what stakeholders to attract and for
designing the contest. In turn, the goals will be affected by the stakeholders
involved as well as the available design options. This will then affect what information technology structure is needed to facilitate transfer of knowledge and
information between the stakeholders.

4.2.1 Set Goals

The organiser's goals are fundamental to the design and preparation which will be
made later when setting up the contest. In this activity, the organisers establish
goals for open innovation driven by the contests. The goals shape the process and
criteria used to select winning contributions and the assessment of the contest as a
whole. They also provide insights into the role that the organiser will take after the
contest and they therefore govern the strategy the organiser will develop for the post
contest phase.

4.2.2   *Engage Stakeholders*

Key contest stakeholders are: organiser, external developer as well as resource provider and beneficiary. In this activity, the organisers establish an organising team and attract external developers to participate in the contest. Moreover, the organisers attract providers of necessary resources, and they clarify who the beneficiaries are, for example end-users and the organisers themselves.

4.2.3   *Design Contest*

There are several ways to design a contest. In this activity, the organisers design the contest based on the goals and the stakeholders it is supposed to attract. Media, contest period and task specificity are examples of design elements covered in this activity.

4.2.4   *Develop Platform*

Open digital innovation requires that knowledge and information is transferred prior to, during and after the innovation contest. It also requires that knowledge transfer is coordinated by the organising team. In this activity, the organisers establish a contest support platform that supports digital service development and enables effective communication between external and internal stakeholders during the innovation process.

4.2.5   *Monitor Contest*

In addition to the four activities described above, the activity *Monitor contest* starts in this phase and extends across all the three phases of the approach. The organisers monitor and assess the progress of the contest and its effects. It includes a method for developing a measurement model specific to the goals of a particular contest.

4.3   The Contest Phase

The heart of the approach is the contest phase. In this phase the organiser moves from planning and preparation to contest operations. It starts with the activity *Motivate developers* to attract participants to the contest. Organising innovation as a contest may seem simple, however, it requires careful management. This need for management is addressed in the activity *Manage operations*. A contest is about picking winners given a pre-defined set of rules. In the last activity, *Evaluate contributions*, the submitted service prototypes are evaluated following the assessment process defined in the pre-contest phase.

4.3.1 Motivate Developers

A successful contest requires the participation of external developers. In this activity, the organisers engage, enrol and motivate participants. For some contests, the threshold to participate is low, which enables the organisers to attract external developers from various target groups. In other cases, the threshold to participate is high due to the requirements of a specific domain knowledge or technical expertise. Given the circumstances for the specific contest, one key activity is to motivate and engage individuals or teams of developers to participate.

4.3.2 Manage Operations

Operating an open digital innovation contest is a delicate project. The activity *Manage operations* is informed by the project management body of knowledge. In this activity, the organisers coordinate the distributed work process, involving several stakeholders, from the contest start to the final when the winners are selected. It involves proactive and reactive measures to common problems.

4.3.3 Evaluate Contribution

There are several ways to run the winners in a contest. In this activity, the organisers develop evaluation criteria from the contest goals. Moreover, the organisers choose and apply a method for evaluating contest contributions. For example, they can establish an expert-jury or use a peer-review method. The mapping of evaluation criteria to the goals is defined for the contest.

4.4 The Post-contest Phase

Organisers' involvement in the contest process does not necessarily end with the final and singling out of winners. Given the goals of a specific contest and its intended effects, an organiser could be more or less involved also after the contest.

Based on a framework of different options for post-contest support, in the activity *Develop strategy, the* organisers develop a strategy for involvement after the contest. The activity *Manage barriers* addresses barriers that hamper external developers when they move from the prototype development to the service deployment. In the activity *Design business model*, organisers design new or adapt existing business models for the decided strategy.

4.4.1   Develop Strategy

Organisers can decide to be more or less involved in the aftermath of a contest. In the activity *Develop strategy*, organisers choose between a number of strategic options for their relationships with former contest participants based on different types of open innovation. Which strategy to develop depends on the organiser's goals. The activity includes a framework of strategic options, from no involvement to actively deploying services in a market.

4.4.2   Manage Barriers

To deploy a service prototype requires additional development efforts. During this effort, external developers will face a number of barriers. In this activity, the organisers can support the developers by identifying barriers and coping with them. It includes a framework of barriers common to external developers and suggestions for coping strategies.

4.4.3   Design Business Model

Organisers involvement in service deployment will affect their business models in various ways. For example, by continuing to publish open data used during the contest, the organiser will become a data provider. In the activity *Design business model*, the organisers investigate the business impact of their chosen strategy for post-contest support, and they determine if and how their business model should be adapted.

Chapter 5
Set Contest Goals

Abstract This chapter deals with contest goals. First, different types of goals are presented together with examples from different contests. Then the activity *Set goals* is described with guidelines and a running example. This important activity in the pre-contest phase affects and is itself affected by several of the other activities in the approach, such as *Engage stakeholders* and *Design contest*. Finally, we suggest further reading on the use of goals to support management.

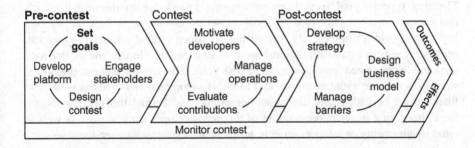

Organisations arrange digital innovations contests for several reasons. As described in Chap. 3, they can help to generate ideas that can be transformed into products and services. They can help to select between competing ideas and filter out those that are most promising. They can also help to improve the visibility and image of the organiser by creating a buzz and drawing attention to the organiser and its brands. Yet another purpose is to strengthen the size and dynamism of an innovation community in which the organiser participates. For open digital innovation contests, a related purpose is to investigate the opportunities that an open data platform can offer an innovation community. Feedback from an innovation contest can then help the organiser to understand which of the data offered is seen as the most useful by the developers, what additional data could be valuable and which delivery channels are most appropriate.

© Springer International Publishing AG 2017

A. Hjalmarsson et al., *Open Digital Innovation*, Progress in IS,

DOI 10.1007/978-3-319-56339-8_5

5.1 Types of Goals

Although goals vary between contests, the overall goal of organisers of open digital innovation contests is to drive forward innovation of viable digital services using open data. To this end, there are three types of goals found in open digital innovation contests. These types of goals are linked to the three open innovation process archetypes developed by Gassmann and Enkel (2004). The first type of goal relates to the outside-in process of bringing in external knowledge to support the organisation's innovation. The second type of goal is associated with the inside-out process of transferring ideas for exploitation outside the organisation. The third type of goal refers to the coupled process of innovating in alliances with complementary partners. In addition, organisers of open digital innovation contests can have other types of goals not related to innovation, such as increasing the organisation's brand image. In Table 5.1 the different types and examples of goals from open digital innovation contests are presented.

5.1.1 Outside-In Type of Goal

The first type of goal is to bring in external knowledge to the organisation's innovation process. This type of goal is set to overcome a lack of internal knowledge and resources. By organising an open digital innovation contest, organisers aim to establish relationships with external developers and to integrate the knowledge gained from co-operating with them. Through the contest, organisers want to harness external creativity and to use development resources as well as to filter out the best ideas and digital service prototypes. During this process, organisers also gain a better understanding of the needs of open data sources as well as what requirements developers have in terms of data quality and service levels.

Table 5.1 Types of goals of digital innovation contests with examples

Type of Goal	Goals
Outside-in	• Harness creativity beyond organisational boundaries
	• Attract development resources outside the organisation
	• Increase understanding of open data needs and requirements
	• Filter ideas
Inside-out	• Increase awareness of societal and commercial challenges where open data and digital services can be used
	• Solve societal and commercial challenges through the development and use of digital services
	• Increase interest for and use of open data
Coupled	• Attract and engage community members
	• Foster complementation through platform strategy
Non-innovation	• Strengthen organisation's brand

In general, contests are used in the early stages of innovation to stimulate the generation of ideas and service prototypes through the innovative use and transformation of open data. For example, the Open Stockholm Award was used to encourage external developers to offer new digital services under the umbrella of the City of Stockholm without hiring them.

5.1.2 Inside-Out Type of Goal

The second type of goal is to transfer ideas and resources to be exploited by external developers. Organisers can use digital innovation contests to make available open data and to direct attention to problems that can be overcome by developing digital services that make use of these open data resources. Another goal that organisations have when organising contests is to increase the interest and use of their open data sources. Although the availability of open data increases, partly stimulated by political decisions such as the PSI directive, the awareness and use of these sources are still low. Therefore, organisers are often interested in increasing the use of the open data they provide and the platform they use to support developers. For example, the organisers of Travelhack and the owners of Trafiklab, see Chap. 3, wanted to increase the interest among external developers for open data related to public transport.

5.1.3 Coupled Type of Goals

The third type of goal is to work in alliances with complementary partners where deep interaction is necessary for successful innovation. In this case, the contest can provide the means for strengthening an innovation community to which the organiser belongs and to stimulate the use of a platform that supports forming alliances and interaction between developers. For example, one of the goals of Travelhack 2013 was to double the number of community members of Trafiklab.

5.1.4 Non-innovation Type of Goal

The fourth type of goal is to use digital innovation contests to achieve ends not directly related to innovation. A common goal is to use contests for marketing purposes to strengthen the brand image of the organiser. For example, the City of Stockholm used the Open Stockholm Award, see Chap. 3, to strengthen its image as a modern high-tech city.

5.2   Relationships Between Types of Goals

If we look closer at the different goal types, we find that they can be interrelated. Organisers can use inside-out types of goals to stimulate outside-in types of goals and vice versa. For example, by providing open data and ideas for solutions to innovation challenges, organisers can stimulate external developers to contribute with their knowledge, skills and creativity. Also coupled types of goals can be used to stir up action with both inside-out and outside-in types of goals. For example, close collaboration on an innovation shared among partners may lead to the development of new knowledge inside the organisation which, in turn, can help it to move the locus of innovation to inside the organisation.

5.3   Why Are Goals Needed?

Goals are an important part of planning and controlling the process of digital innovation contests. Using goals is a rational and analytical approach where the goals help with designing the contest and in planning the other activities of the digital innovation process. Stakeholders' commitments to goals help in converging efforts to meet deadlines and to achieve goals. After plans have been made, stakeholders can take the goals as given which supports stability and provides a sense of purpose. However, it is important to understand that different stakeholders have different goals and engage in organising digital innovation contests for various reasons. This means that the goal setting activity must, on the one hand, support goal setting for the planning of the innovation contest itself and, on the other hand, provide a basis for stakeholders to manage individual goals relative to the common goals of the digital innovation contest and in relation to the other stakeholders' goals. For example, the common goal of all the organisers of an innovation contest could be to stimulate the development of e-Health services, while the individual goal for one of the organisers could be to establish relationships with skilled service developers.

5.4   Activity Description

The activity *Set goals* aims at formulating goals for the digital innovation contest, e.g., to increase the influx of novel ideas into an organisation. Several stakeholders: companies, public organisations, interest groups and individuals, may be involved in organising an innovation contest and it is important to clarify the goals for each stakeholder. Typically, this activity would start with discussions with one stake-holder or in discussions between small numbers of stakeholders. The discussions would revolve around innovation challenges and opportunities with organising an open digital innovation contest. Here Table 5.1 provides a checklist for organisers when setting goals. Between this activity and the activity *Attract stakeholders*, stakeholders are successively identified and subsequently involved in goal discussions. Moreover, based on the chosen format in the activity *Design contest*, some contest goals will be given. The activity is completed when all stakeholders have agreed on the contest goals and resolved any conflicts between their respective individual goals. Conflicts between the goals need to be managed in this activity, e.g., by the use of goal modelling and conflict resolution techniques. The output of this activity is a common goal statement for the contest supported by all stakeholders.

5.4.1 Sub-activities

1. Identify innovation challenges and classify as:
   (a) Lack of internal knowledge
   (b) Lack of external exploitation of ideas and resources
   (c) Lack of close interaction with complementary partners.

2. Set goals to satisfy the innovation challenges:
   (a) Outside-in types of goals
   (b) Inside-out types of goals
   (c) Coupled types of goals.

3. Set non-innovation types of goals to satisfy other types of challenges, for example, related to marketing.
4. Formulate a common goal statement shared by all stakeholders.

5.5 Running Example

In the case of the Rio Transport Challenge, the goal discussion started as a governmental collaboration between Brazil and Sweden with the aim of stimulating innovation. One initiative was to arrange an open digital innovation contest with organisers from both countries. The general goal was to improve public transport in the City of Rio de Janeiro during and after the Olympics. Several stakeholders were involved, including the City of Rio de Janeiro and local transport companies as well as Swedish public agencies, IT-companies and research institutes. The common goals included:

1. Outside-in type of goal: make Rio public transport and urban sustainable mobility more reliable, comfortable and accessible by designing open digital services in three areas: travel planner, comfort and accessibility and experience the Olympics.

2. Inside-out type of goal: exploit the open data sources made available by the City of Rio de Janeiro and its subsidiaries.
3. Coupled type of goal: enable close co-operation between the City of Rio de Janeiro and its subsidiaries and digital service providers through an open data platform supporting data extraction and service provisioning.

There were no non-innovation types of goals defined for the contest. Finally, the goals were documented and communicated via the contest website.

5.6   Guidelines

Setting goals for open digital innovation contests is no different from setting goals in other management situations. This means that widely available guidelines such as the SMART framework and guidelines for managing collaboration are also applicable when managing contests. However, we have found that when managing innovation contests, organisers can get lost in the multitude of innovation and non-innovation types of goals and expectations that different stakeholders can have by being involved in organising contests. Therefore, our recommendation is to focus on the innovation problem driving the need for the contest and to make sure to set goals for a tangible output in the form of, at least, prototypes of digital services. Then all the other goals can be organised as sub-goals to this goal or as goals complementing this innovation focused goal.

Guideline:

– Align contest goals with innovation goals that are strategic for the stakeholders!
– Make sure to set challenging contest goals to drive innovation forward!

5.7   Read More

Managing with goals has a long history and is intimately related to strategic management as well as project management. Peter Drucker in his book, The Practice of Management (1954) launched the term Management by Objectives (MBO). MBO is the idea that managers and employees define goals and then use these goals to evaluate performance. These goals can then be used as the starting point for strategic planning.

The use of goals and objectives to support management includes goal setting, involvement of employees in goal formulation, feedback and performance related remuneration. Well-known techniques include, apart from Management by Objectives, Performance Measurement and Balanced Scorecard. However, it may be difficult to apply these techniques and the use of pre-defined goals on technology driven entrepreneurial ventures and in the context of innovation management. Also, the decision making of entrepreneurs tends not to focus on particular goals and the selection of the resources needed to reach the goals. Rather, entrepreneurs start with a general idea that becomes more and more precise as the venture unfolds; this is referred to as effectuation (Sarasvathy 2001). These entrepreneurs tend to regard goals as emerging rather than given. Also decision makers who find themselves in unpredictable environments may find it difficult to use predefined goals since (i) corporate goals may be difficult to envision and (ii) employees would be reluctant to negotiate targets when goal attainment is influenced by factors that are hard for employees to influence. However, Chiesa and Frattini (2007) argue that performance measurement in the context of R&D is valuable for obtaining a variety of objectives such as supporting decision-making, motivating personnel and fostering organisational learning. Moreover, goals are important to support collaboration between partners involved in joint innovation, such as organising open digital innovation contests. Finally, goals support monitoring and evaluation which is an important element of organisational learning.

References

Chiesa, V., & Frattini, F. (2007). Exploring the differences in performance measurement between research and development: Evidence from a multiple case study. *R&D Management, 37*(4), 283–301.

Drucker, P. F. (1954). *The practice of management.* New York: Harper Brothers.

Gassmann, O., & Enkel, E. (2004). Towards a theory of open innovation: Three core process archetypes. *Proceedings of the R&D Management Conference,* Lisbon, Portugal, July 6–9.

Sarasvathy, S. D. (2001). Causation and effectuation: Toward a theoretical shift from economic inevitability to entrepreneurial contingency. *Academy of Management Review, 26*(2), 243–263.

Chapter 6
Engage Contest Stakeholders

Abstract This chapter address the stakeholders that should be identified and engaged in the contest process. First, different types of stakeholders are presented along with their characteristics and support to the contest organizers. This is followed by a description of the activity *Engage contest stakeholders* and a running example. Engaging contest stakeholders is affected by the activity *Set goals* and itself affects activities such as *Motivate developers* and *Design contest*. Often, iterations are made between engaging stakeholders and the process to design the contest, as the structure of the competition is evolving during the pre-contest phase. Finally, we suggest further reading on engaging stakeholders in open digital innovation.

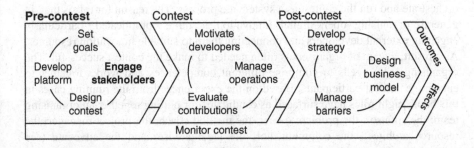

Engage contest stakeholders is the second activity in the pre-contest phase. Open digital innovation contests are seldom organised by a single organisation. Instead collaboration between partners is often needed. The partners required to organise a contest are, however, not necessarily fully engaged from the start. Through the process of setting contest goals, see Chap. 5, it will become apparent what partners are needed in order to organise the contest successfully. Setting the goals will also decide what types of participants, i.e. external developers, should be engaged in the contest. Organisers and participants are thus two key stakeholders in the contest. Other key stakeholders are resource providers, for example, open data providers

Fig. 6.1 Four key contest
stakeholders

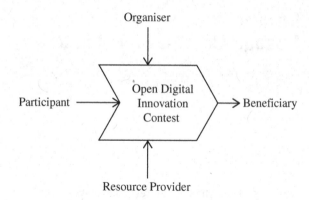

and prize sponsors, as well as beneficiaries, i.e. stakeholders who have an interest in the outcome of the contest. We summarise the four key contest stakeholders in Fig. 6.1.

6.1 Organizer

Open digital innovation contests require one or several organisers who design, orchestrate and run the contest as a systematic process. The reason for this is that, in general, organising open digital innovation is quite complicated, particularly engaging external developers and connecting them to suitable innovation resources. As a result, a team of organisers is often needed to make the contest successful. The organising team needs to comprise different competences and works together to encourage contest participants. Based on the experiences from the running cases in this book, eight roles have surfaced as candidates for putting together an organising team: the sponsor, the problem owner, the method coach, the project manager, the resource architect, the communicator, the legal adviser and the advocate (see Table 6.1). These roles can be staffed with individuals from one or several organisations.

Sponsor. A *sponsor* is responsible for taking key decisions about the contest and has the ultimate financial responsibility. If there are several organisers, then there could be several sponsors. They will then form the steering group of the contest.

Problem owner. A *problem owner* is responsible for identifying contest challenges. The challenges identified by the problem owners are the basis for the contest goals, see Chap. 5. The main expertise that problem owners bring to the organising team is knowledge about the domain that the contest addresses. For example, in the Olympic City Transport Challenge, a problem owner from a transport research institute identified the main public transport problems in Rio de Janeiro that the contest should address. If the contest addresses multiple challenges that transcend a specific organisation, the role of the problem owner is often shared by several organisations.

Table 6.1 Example of roles, role characteristics and contributions to an organising team

Sub-type	Characteristic(s)	Examples of contribution(s)
Sponsor	Decides about the contest and has ultimate financial responsibility	Contest challenge ownership
Problem owner	Responsible for identifying and formulating contest challenge(s)	Domain knowledge
Method coach	Contest design and operation expertise	Contest method Contest rules
Project manager	Project management and operational staff	Operational leadership Contest coordination Contest administration
Resource architect	Definition and supply of appropriate contest resources	Enables digital resources Ensures a good fit between contest objectives and resources available
Communicator	Contest marketing and communications	Marketing of the contest Recruitment of external developers (participants)
Legal adviser	Proprietary interest advice, intellectual property guidance, general regulatory assistance	Intellectual property aspects Contest rules
Advocate	Liaison person between the organising team and potential participants and potential contest beneficiaries	Links to potential participants (e.g. students) Motivates beneficiaries to contribute to the contest

Method coach. The main responsibility of the *method coach* is to support the organising team to develop the contest design and operation process. The method coach aims to increase understanding of how open digital contests are arranged to meet established goals. This is done through providing a suitable contest method.

Project manager. In order to prepare and operate the contest as a project, the team also requires a *project manager*. The project manager provides management procedures to the contest process, as well as coordination tasks throughout its operations.

Resource architect. A *resource architect* defines what resources are needed. This could include open data, open data services and static digitised resources. Also, a resource architect determines how to make resources accessible and facilitates the interaction with resource providers. Resources are often provided through a contest platform, see Chap. 8.

Communicator. A *communicator* is responsible for systematic communication to different internal and external stakeholders. Important tasks include recruiting participants and creating media coverage of the contest.

Legal adviser. The *legal adviser* provides advice on the distribution of legal property rights among stakeholders, including participants and resource providers. The legal adviser supports the development of the contest rules, e.g. who will own the contest results and how they can be used after the contest. Furthermore, the legal adviser is involved in establishing rules for who should be eligible to participate and what the rules for awarding or claiming the prizes are.

Advocate. An *advocate* facilitates interaction between participants and representatives of beneficiaries. Advocates can ensure that a contest attracts appropriate external developers and that they can manage development barriers after the contest is finished.

6.2 Participant

Open digital innovation organised as a contest requires participants in order to succeed. These participants are external developers, i.e., they do not belong to the contest organisers. Five types of participants may be attracted to a contest: citizens, community developers, students, entrepreneurial developers and professional developers, see Table 6.2.

The contest goals determine what types of participants should be targeted. If the goals are inclusive and address a domain that is easy to understand and contribute to, then a broad mix of participants can be engaged in the contest. However, if the goals are exclusive and address a domain difficult to understand and contribute to, then it may be better to engage a narrower mix or a specific group of participants. Also, experience shows that the key motives for participation differ between the participant types. This will in turn affect the contest design, with respect to the prize and other design elements, see Chaps. 7 and 9.

Citizen. A *citizen* is a member of the general public. The main motive for citizens to participate is to contribute to the society by solving a problem or a

Table 6.2 *Participant types and characteristics*

Participant type	Characteristics
Citizen	– Member of the general public – May lack software development skills
Community developer	– Develops software solutions as a hobby – Engaged in software communities
Student	– Engaged in academic education – Able to develop software solutions
Entrepreneurial developer	– Highly skilled in software development – Driven by commercial motives – Belongs to a loosely connected team of developers or a start-up company
Professional developer	– Highly skilled in software development – Belongs to an established firm who sponsor participation in the contest

challenge in a use domain. However, citizens may lack necessary understanding to innovate in use domains dependent on complex systems and technology. The best effect from including citizens is therefore achieved when the contest addresses a use domain close to citizens' everyday life situations. Furthermore, it is helpful to mix citizens with other developer types to add user experience to the participating teams.

Community developer. A *community developer* is a citizen who has software development as a hobby, is able to develop software solutions and is engaged in software communities. For example, the Swedish Trafiklab hosts a community of developers for open transport data.

Student. A *student* is a citizen who is engaged in academic education, for example in informatics or business administration. Involving individual students or teams of students in contests is a great opportunity to establish partnerships between universities and industry. However, such collaboration has to be initiated early and be carefully managed, as it requires that multiple goals, both academic and industry related, be aligned and met through the contest. To achieve large-scale participation of student teams, the organisers should, at an early stage, engage an advocate, for example a university teacher.

Entrepreneurial developer. An *entrepreneurial developer* is driven by commercial motives but has not yet established an organisational setting to pursue an entrepreneurial endeavour. An entrepreneurial developer often belongs to a loosely connected team of developers organised as a start-up or a network. Entrepreneurial developers are often highly skilled in software development, but they lack the support and management resources available to professional developers.

Professional developer. A *professional developer* belongs to an established firm and represents the organisation when participating in the contest. The participation is sponsored by management who have made an active decision that the organisation should be part of the contest.

6.3 Resource Provider

Open digital innovation contests aim to generate digital service prototypes that are both innovative and solid. An important condition for achieving this is that the participants are provided with appropriate building blocks, which are used in combination with the participants' own resources. The provision of building blocks is not given. Appropriate resources need to be identified and they have to be provided by someone. Consequently, the organising team has to decide what building blocks should be provided and by whom. To stress this, the organising team should include a resource architect, see Table 6.1, who can lead the work to: (1) define what resources are needed, (2) define who should provide the building blocks, (3) adapt the building blocks to meet the contest goals, (4) ensure that the building blocks are provided to the participants during the contest via the contest support platform and (5) estimate the costs for providing the building blocks to the participants.

There are different types of resource providers, see Table 6.3. They can make the resources available only during the contest, or they can make them generally available and not limited to the contest. The provision could be internal, that is, provided by the organisers of the contest. It could also be external and provided by organisations not affiliated to the contest. Provision of resources could be active for the contest purpose or it could be done passively. Active provision means that resources are made available and adapted by the resource provider for the contest purpose. Passive provision means that the resource provider simply makes available resources without adapting them to the contest objectives. Financial resources could be provided directly to the participants or handled by the organisers and used to operate the contest.

Table 6.3 Types of resource providers, characteristics and examples of contributions

Resource provider type	Characteristics	Examples of contributions
Provider of open digitised knowledge	An organisation that provides knowledge that has been digitised to facilitate external developers to innovate	Description of needs Description of requests Description of vision Description of system, organisation or location
Provider of open data	An organisation that provides one or several data sets to be used by external developers to build on	Real-time data Static data Signals from vehicles or systems
Provider of open digital services	An organisation that provides one or several adaptable and/or accessible digital services to build on	Accessible services, not adaptable to plugin to the prototype Accessible services, free to adapt and plugin to the prototype
Provider of open digital platform	An organisation that provides an expandable system with key functionality accessible for external developers to build new services on	Accessible interfaces to connect new digital services Core functionality shared by different digital services
Provider of open support tools	An organisation that provides one or more tools to facilitate external developers to innovate	Software developer kit, business case toolbox Development environment Testing environment Simulator, visualise prototype
Provider of financial resources	An organisation that provides financial resources to the open digital innovation contest	Reward sponsorship Operational funding Resource financing

6.4 Beneficiary

Beneficiaries have an interest in the outcome of a contest. There are several types, see Table 6.4.

Organiser. Open digital innovation contests are organised to develop innovative and solid digital service prototypes that meet the organiser's objectives. A key beneficiary of the outcomes of a contest is thus the organiser. This organisation could either benefit directly, as the outcome addresses a specific problem, or

Table 6.4 Types of beneficiaries, characteristics and examples of benefits

Sub-type	Characteristic(s)	Examples of benefit(s) received
Organiser	Organisers can benefit directly or indirectly by the output of the open digital innovation contest	Direct: outcome that solves a direct problem; new relationships between participants are established; exposure; competitive advantage Indirect: an outcome that solves a problem for another stakeholder that in turn creates value for the problem owner
End-user	End-users may benefit immediately by the output if the contest output is ready and launched on to a market. End-users may benefit long-term if the contest output reaches an end-user market after it has been transformed into a solution	Immediate: the solution is complete when the contest ends and is launched on an end-user market Overtime: the solution requires adaptation and further development during a post-contest phase in order to be able to launch it on an end-user market
Participant	Participants can benefit directly by the output of the open digital contest	Potential reward Competitive advantage Enhanced idea/prototype Business opportunities Exposure New relationships Experience
Resource provider	Resource providers can benefit directly and/or indirectly by the output of the open digital contest	Direct: resources are being used; feedback on the resources made available to the developers; return on investment Indirect: an outcome that solves a problem for another stakeholder that in turn creates value for the resource provider
Innovation system	Open digital innovation can provide different benefits to stakeholders in an innovation system where the contest is operated (e.g. a city, region, industry, sector)	Innovation output Knowledge and competence enhancement Business value creation Public value creation Societal benefits

indirectly by addressing a problem that another stakeholder has, which, in turn, creates benefits for the organiser.

End-user. End-users can receive immediate value from the contest or value over time depending on the readiness of the solutions from the contest. If the solutions are complete and ready to launch after the contest, then the impact may be immediate to end-users. However, if the solution requires further development or the participants lack the necessary funding, end-users might have to wait before receiving the benefits.

Participant. Participants are also beneficiaries of the innovation contest. Participants can be directly benefitted by the output of the digital contest, adhering to the motives that they have for participating in the process. Benefits could be prizes and rewards they receive, but also enhancements of the service they develop. Business opportunities can surface as a consequence of the contest and new business relationships can be formed. Participation can also improve competences, such as teamwork and technical competences, as well as improving the corporate brand and creating job opportunities.

Resource provider. The resource provider can receive value directly or indirectly from making resources available. One direct benefit is that resources provided are being used to innovate new services and products. It is important for most resource providers to show a high level of use and contests can stimulate the use of data. Another benefit is that the resources will be evaluated by the participants and resource providers can thus receive feedback on the resources they provide. Organisations that provide financial resources will expect a return on their investment.

Innovation system. The last example of a beneficiary type are the people who are part of an innovation system where the contest is operated (e.g. a city, region, industry, sector). Such benefits may be innovation output, knowledge and competence enhancement, business value creation as solutions are turned into business, public value creation as challenges for citizens or communities are addressed, societal benefits as environmental or social sustainability may be strengthened as a consequence of the output from the contest.

6.5 Activity Description

The activity: *Engage contest stakeholders* is conducted in two steps. The first step is based on the contest's goals and aims to identify and involve organisers in the organising team as well as to identify beneficiaries of the contest and their expectations. The second step is based on the contest design and determines what participants should be engaged in the contest and what resource providers are needed. Hence, this activity is closely interrelated with the activities *Set goals*, *Design contest* and *Motivate developers*.

6.5.1 Sub-activities

1. Review the contest goals.
2. Engage an appropriate organising team, including:

    a. roles that should be included in the team
    b. organisations that should staff the roles in the team
    c. division of responsibilities between roles and organisations.

3. Engage beneficiaries from the types presented in Table 6.4 and for each:

    a. identify benefits
    b. analyse expectations.

4. Review the contest design.
5. Determine types of participants who should be engaged, see Table 6.2.
6. Engage resource providers based on the resource needs of the contest design.

6.6 Running Example

Sponsorship and problem ownership in Travelhack 2013 was shared between two public organisations. Their goals were to increase the attractiveness of public transport and attract more citizens to use such transport modes. Besides acting as sponsors and problem owners, they also shared the resource architect function and thus decided what resources the participants should use in the contest. They also ensured that financial resources were in place to design and operate the contest. A non-profit making organisation, with extensive knowledge of open digital innovation and contest methodology, was included in the organising team to provide advice on how to organise the contest. Also, a consultancy company was engaged to provide project management and to coordinate communication. No specific legal adviser was brought into join the team, but the sponsors used their legal departments to review the contest rules and the public regulations for providing prizes.

The organising team was engaged in the Spring of 2012 and started working in August 2012. The team worked intensively to prepare the contest until the contest was launched in January 2013 when preparation was transferred into operational management of the contest.

Travelhack 2013 was advertised as an open innovation contest with no limitations for participation. It comprised an idea phase, where everyone interested in building digital service prototypes to enhance the attractiveness of public transport in Stockholm, was invited. In total, fifty-three teams, with up to five members, participated and twenty-four of these teams were invited to a subsequent prototype phase and a concluding hackathon.

The organising team behind Travelhack 2013 succeeded in creating a contest design that engaged external developers from all the participant types presented in Table 6.2. Community teams competed with entrepreneurial teams and student teams. Also mixed teams participated, for example, citizens formed teams with professional and community developers.

To engage different types of teams, a design decision was made by the organising team on who to engage in the contest. In order to succeed, they developed prizes that would generate a strong interest to participate. The prizes ranged from physical prizes, to a trip to the USA to visit Disrupt in California.[1] The contest was also organised with the intention that the developers, during the final event, had the opportunity to build relationships with stakeholders in the industry and venture capital was invited to the final to help participants present their ideas to potential sponsors.

The main beneficiaries of the contest were (1) the society as a whole represented by the problem owners and their current and future customers using public transport and (2) the participants themselves, as the contest was aimed at encouraging the development of prototypes, which the developers could transform into services ready to be launched on the markets after the contest.

Resources made available were open data in terms of static and dynamic public transport data provided by the problem owners via the open data platform Trafiklab and open APIs. Other available open data sources were advertised to the participants by organisations with an interest in public transport. The relevance of the resources provided was ensured by connecting the advertised data to the contest goals. By doing so, the problem owners showed that they believed that innovative services could be developed on these data. The teams were also encouraged to use alternative data sources not promoted by the contest, as long as the participants used open sources that could be reviewed by the organising team. The organising team also provided support tools for the participants as well as internal and external financial resources to run the contest.

6.7   Read More

This chapter is based on the notion of 'stakeholder' (Freeman 1984). A stakeholder is "any group or individual who is affected by or can affect the achievement of an organizations objectives" (Freeman 1984, p. 5). Although a contest is not a permanent organisation, the four identified stakeholder types in Fig. 6.1 can be affected by and can affect the achievement of an innovation contest. The four types of

---

[1] https://techcrunch.com/events/disrupt-sf-2013/event-info/.

stakeholders have different goals with contests and therefore need to be treated differently. Moreover, by not paying attention to all stakeholders, organisers might risk the success of the contest.

Reference

Freeman, R. E. (1984). *Strategic management: A stakeholder approach*. Boston: Pitman.

Chapter 7
Design Contest

Abstract In this chapter, we discuss how to design an open digital innovation contest. First, contest formats are matched to contest goals. Then, different elements of contest design are presented, followed by a description of the activity *Design contest* with guidelines and a running example. *Design contest* sets the scene for the remainder of the contest process and is heavily affected by the activity *Set goals*. Finally, contest rules and how to budget a contest are discussed together with some suggestions for further reading.

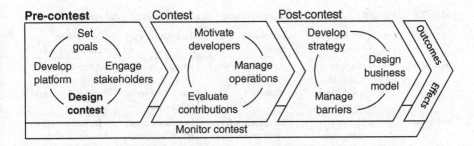

An open digital innovation contest must be actively designed to meet its goals. The organisers have a number of ingredients, or design elements, at their disposal and their combination determines whether the contest will be successful or not. In Chap. 3 we distinguished between different kinds of contests based on the variables, time and participation. By varying time, the output of a contest can be controlled. Short contests stimulate creativity and are often used to generate ideas quickly, but sometimes they are not good at producing solid service prototypes. Long contests stimulate more rigorous development cycles and are often used to create mature and solid prototypes close to market implementation. Similarly, organisers can control participation so that the results are more or less homogeneous. Organisers use inclusive contests to stimulate a wide variety of results, while they use exclusive contests, with carefully selected participants, to direct the results to certain areas.

Based on these two variables, there are four different kinds of contests. An innovation jam is short in time and very inclusive; it is useful for generating many new ideas. An innovation cup is also inclusive but is extended in time; it is helpful for strengthening an innovation community. An innovation battle is short and exclusive; it can be used for quickly identifying strong opportunities. An innovation challenge is long and exclusive; it can help an organiser to decide whether to build or to buy.

Given the goal of an open digital contest, it is possible to choose a contest format. At first glance all contest formats seem to work for all the goal types, but a closer look reveals that some contest formats are more supportive for some goal types and less supportive for others. For outside-in goals, where organisers aim to bring in external knowledge to support the organisation's innovation, all four formats work but will yield different results, see Table 7.1. An Innovation Jam will attract many ideas in a short period of time, but there is a great risk that the resulting prototypes will be less solidly relevant for the organiser. For example, an Innovation Jam could be used if an open data provider wants to increase knowledge about open data needs and requirements. An Innovation Battle will, on the other hand, result in more relevant prototypes but they will still be less solid and far from able to be implemented. An Innovation Cup will take a longer time to conduct but

Table 7.1 Summary of differences between contest formats for different goal types

	Innovation jam	Innovation battle	Innovation cup	Innovation challenge
Outside-in	Attracts many less solid ideas	Attracts a few more relevant ideas	Attracts many ideas and filters out a few more solid ideas	Attracts a few more relevant and solid ideas
Inside-out	Develops many less solid ideas available for exploitation by anyone interested	Develops a few, more relevant ideas which are available for exploitation by anyone interested	Develops many ideas and filters out a few more solid ideas available for exploitation by anyone interested	Develops a few, more relevant and solid ideas that the expert participant can implement or transfer to another party for exploitation
Coupled	Not applicable	Not applicable	Develops relationships with several developers with skills that complement their own	Develops relationships with a small number of experts with skills that complement their own
Non-innovation	Market their brand to a broad audience	Market their brand to a select audience	Not applicable	Not applicable

Table 7.2 Summary of choices for selecting a contest format

	Innovation jam	Innovation battle	Innovation cup	Innovation challenge
Amount of ideas	High	Low	High	Low
Solidity	Low	Low	High	High
Relevance	Low	High	Low	High
Time frame	Short	Short	Long	Long
Audience	Broad and diverse	Narrow and expert orientated	Broad and diverse	Narrow and expert orientated

still result in many ideas and, through the different filtering steps, the prototypes will be more solid and closer to implementation. However, an Innovation Challenge will, due to the participating experts, result in more relevant prototypes closer to implementation. For example, an Innovation Challenge could be used when an organiser has a good knowledge of the problem but lacks the technical competence to develop viable service options for solving the problem.

For inside-out goals, the different contest formats will also lead to different results. Innovation Jams can be used by organisers who, within a short time frame, want to attract many ideas and make them available for exploitation, either by the participant or by another interested party. For coupled goals aiming for innovation in alliances with complementary partners, only two of the contest formats are recommended. For other types of goals, not related to innovation, all of the contest formats may be applicable.

Table 7.2 includes a summary of the different choices the organisers have in terms of selecting the contest format that best matches their goals.

7.1 Designing a Contest Based on a Contest Format

Once the contest format has been chosen, it is time to design the contest in more detail. There are a large number of options available when designing a contest. These options can be expressed by means of *design elements*, see Chap. 3. The idea with design elements is that the organisers of innovation contests use them as variables to configure the design of their specific contest. By varying the values of design elements, organisers are able to design digital innovation contests that meet their specific goals and are more likely to have the intended effects. Figure 7.1 presents a comparison of the design of more than thirty digital innovation contests.

Below we classify the design elements in three different categories. In the first category, we find design elements that are given by the contest format. In the second category we find general design elements that are either obvious or inherent in the definition of an open digital innovation contest. The third category includes

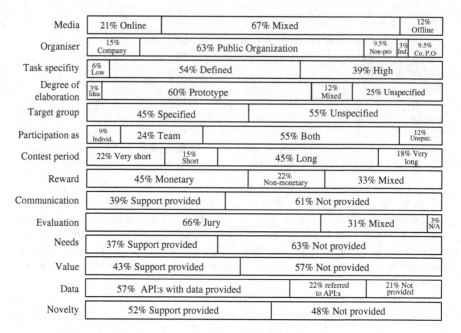

Media	21% Online	67% Mixed			12% Offline
Organiser	15% Company	63% Public Organization		9.5% Non-pro	3% Ind. / 9.5% Co. P.O
Task specifity	6% Low	54% Defined		39% High	
Degree of elaboration	3% Idea	60% Prototype	12% Mixed	25% Unspecified	
Target group	45% Specified		55% Unspecified		
Participation as	9% Individ.	24% Team	55% Both		12% Unspec.
Contest period	22% Very short	15% Short	45% Long	18% Very long	
Reward	45% Monetary		22% Non-monetary	33% Mixed	
Communication	39% Support provided		61% Not provided		
Evaluation	66% Jury		31% Mixed	3% N/A	
Needs	37% Support provided		63% Not provided		
Value	43% Support provided		57% Not provided		
Data	57% API:s with data provided		22% referred to API:s	21% Not provided	
Novelty	52% Support provided		48% Not provided		

Fig. 7.1 Comparison of design elements between digital innovation contests (Juell-Skielse et al. 2014, p. 254)

design elements that need to be considered irrespective of the chosen contest format.

7.1.1 Design Elements Given by the Contest Format

The first category consists of design elements that are given by the chosen contest format and includes Target group and Contest period.

7.1.1.1 Target Group

The target group includes a specification of the kinds of participants who should be attracted to the contest. For Innovation Battles and Innovation Challenges, the target group is specified. For example, Volvo Cars Challenge only welcomed invited teams from a few selected software development firms. It is also possible to specify certain criteria for entering the contest, like the Olympic City Transport Challenge that required participants to demonstrate previous experience of developing travel planner apps. For Innovation Jams and Innovation Cups the target group is unspecified. By not specifying the target group, the intention is to attract a large number of participants with different competences and experiences. In summary, the options for the design element Target group are:

- Specified target group
- Unspecified target group.

The benefits of specifying a target group are that the organisers control who is participating and know the competences of the participants. By selecting participants, it is possible for organisers to attract individuals with a status in certain communities, which, in turn, will affect the reputation of the digital innovation contest and thereby attract more participants. In this way, organisers can control participation in their contest the better to manage the outcome of the contest. The other approach is not to specify a target group and leave participation open. Although organisers have less control over who will participate, they will attract a broader group of participants. The benefits are that the variation of the outcome may be larger and more creative.

7.1.1.2 Contest Period

Contest period refers to how long a time the digital innovation contest lasts, from very short term to very long term. The contest period does not include the pre-contest phase of planning the contest. A very short term contest could, for example, be a 24-h hackathon, while a very long term contest, for example, could last for six months, as in the case of the Olympic City Transport Challenge. Long term contests are often divided into several stages where filtering can take place after each stage. Short contests trigger ideas and creativity while long contests give room for elaboration and the development of more solid ideas closer to implementation. In summary, the options for the design element Contest period are:

- Very short term, up to a week
- Short term, up to four weeks
- Long term, one to three months
- Very long term, more than three months.

7.1.2 General Design Elements

The second category is comprised of two general design elements including Organiser and Degree of elaboration.

7.1.2.1 Organiser

The contest design is obviously affected by the organisation initiating the contest as well as the other organisations involved in the organising team. Digital innovation contests initiated by public organisations typically focus on generating public value, while companies initiating contests often focus on creating commercial value. As described in Chap. 6, an organising team should involve a number of different roles in order to cope with the complexity of digital innovation contests. These roles can come from one or several organisations. The selection of organisations making up the organising team has a curbing effect on the contest design, i.e. the organisations' competences, resources and brand images will spill over to the contest. For example, a contest organised by IKEA and Volvo will be differently perceived by potential participants than a contest organised by NASA and Google. Therefore, the organisers need to take into account what competences and other resources are necessary for organising the contest, see Table 6.1, and what image they would like to present to the participants. If they find that competences or resources are missing or that the images of the organisers are not in harmony with the goals of the contest, then they should consider involving other organisations in the organising team, see Fig. 7.2.

In summary, the options for the design element Organiser are:

- Company
- Public organisation
- Non-profit-making organisation
- Individual.

Fig. 7.2 Table for analysing how well an organising team's competences, resources and image match the goals of the contest

	Competence and resources vs. contest goals	
Image vs. contest goals	Match	No match
Match	Ok	Add organisation with complementary competences and resources
No match	Add organisation with complementary image	Add organisation with complementary image and competences and resources

7.1.2.2 Degree of Elaboration

Degree of elaboration refers to the type of contribution that is expected from the participants. In our definition of an open digital innovation contest, see Chap. 3, we presume that the contribution is in the form of a prototype of a digital service. However, longer contests might be divided into an idea phase and a prototype phase. In the first phase, the contribution is in the form of a more or less elaborated idea, while, in the second phase, it consists of a prototype of a digital service. Moreover, a prototype could be more or less mature where a less developed prototype is merely a way to demonstrate a service concept, whereas a more mature prototype is closer to an implemented digital service. The degree of elaboration is important to clarify for the participants in order for them to meet the expectations of the contest. One way to influence the degree of elaboration is to give advice about prototyping or to include prototyping tools in the software developer kit, see Chap. 8. The options for Degree of elaboration are:

- Idea
- Sketch
- Concept
- Prototype
- Solution
- Evolving.

7.1.3 Detailed Design Elements

The third category of design elements is comprised of elements that are neither given by the chosen contest format nor obvious or inherent in the definition of open digital innovation contests.

7.1.3.1 Media

Media refers to the environment of the open digital innovation contest. The contest could be carried out either by physical presence, digitally, or as a combination. A 24-h Innovation Jam is typically conducted in a common facility with a physical presence. An Innovation Cup, carried out during a longer period of time, could include a combination of digital and physical activities. For example, in a first digitally enabled stage, service concepts are filtered out and, in a second stage, selected finalists gather to compete in a physical meeting. The options for this design element are:

- Online
- Mixed
- Offline.

7.1.3.2   Task specificity

Task specificity refers to how explicitly and precisely participants' tasks are defined. Generally speaking, with a low task specificity, it is easier to attract a larger and broader group of participants, while contests with a high task specificity attract fewer but more specialised and homogeneous participants. A fundamental aspect of task specificity is the maturity of the problem and the maturity of available solutions. We call this "problem–solution maturity", see Table 7.3. Problem-solution maturity is inspired by the concept of technology readiness (Mankins 1995) and can be used to measure how well defined the problem is and how effective known solutions are to solve the problem. If problem-solution maturity is low, it is difficult to achieve high task specificity. On the other hand, if problem-solution maturity is high, it might be more fruitful for the outcome of a contest that the task is highly specified.

The options for this design element are:

- Low (open task)
- Defined
- High (Specific task).

Participation as:
This design element refers to the number of people forming one entity of participation. There are three options:

- Individual
- Team
- Both.

Table 7.3 Levels of problem-solution maturity

Problem-solution maturity	Description
Very high	Clearly specified and highly acknowledged problem and effective solutions available on the market
High	Specified and acknowledged problem and availability of less effective solutions
Medium	Specified problem and lack of solutions
Low	Unspecified problem and lack of solutions

7.1.3.3 Reward and motivation

Participants can be rewarded and motivated in different ways. As discussed in Chap. 9, external developers are typically motivated to participate in digital innovation contests to have fun and to be intellectually challenged. These are intrinsic motivational factors that come from within the individual. However, monetary rewards could provide a means for continuing development after the contest has ended. And, if the organisers of a contests want to attract established business firms to participate in the contest, then monetary rewards, or even the prospect of them, for example, by getting a contract, become more important. For example, in the Rio Transport Challenge, the reward was the right to use the Olympic City brand to market the service and not a prize sum. There are three options:

- Monetary
- Non-monetary
- Mixed.

7.1.3.4 Community Functionality

As described in Chap. 8, a technical platform provides a number of functionalities, one of these being interaction between participants. The options for this design element show whether community functionality is included in the platform:

- Given
- Not given.

7.1.3.5 Evaluation

Evaluation of contest contributions can take different forms:

- Jury evaluation
- Peer review
- Self-assessment
- Mixed.

  This is further described and discussed in Chap. 11.

7.1.3.6 Post-contest Support

Post-contest support refers to the relationship organisers aim to establish with former participants after the contest is finished. There are several options:

- A. None—resources from contest not available
- B. Data—resources from contest remain available
- C. Contacts—provide information and contacts
- D. Application—provide support to apply for development competence and funding
- E. Development—support development
- F. Provisioning—service provisioning.

Post contest support is further described and discussed in Chap. 12.

7.1.3.7   User Needs

User needs are the means provided by organisers to stimulate participants to develop contest contributions that meet end users' requirements of digital services. The means could be either in the form of facilitation or resources. Through facilitation, organisers support participants to understand better user needs in connection with the contest goals. Organisers can also provide resources in the form of, for example, user personae, scenarios, trends, case descriptions and problem briefs. Options for the design element are:

- Provided
- Not provided.

7.1.3.8   Business Value

Values are means provided to support participants to develop service prototypes that possess the potential to become viable services. Organisers can, for example, provide resources in the form of toolboxes to develop business models and connections to venture capital. Organisers can also offer help to participants to create valuable offers or business models in relation to their service prototypes. For example, organisers can provide workshops or meetings where participants are matched or introduced to business coaches or representatives for venture capital or other business networks. Options are:

- Provided
- Not provided.

7.1.3.9   Data

Data are the developers' honey in open digital service contests. Organisers use different ways to provide participants with relevant data. Many organisers provide their own data and APIs, which are often an integral part of the contest platform and the set of features "Resource Provision Support" described in Chap. 8. Other organisers guide participants to relevant data sources. Options for this design element are:

- APIs with data
- Data sets
- Links to APIs and or data
- Not provided.

7.1.3.10   Innovation Novelty

Novelty means that the outcome from a contest should be more innovative than current services on the market. In order to promote innovation, the organiser could define rules or criteria for intellectual property and evaluation that include novelty. The organiser could also provide an innovation baseline with a review of existing services on the market. Moreover, the organiser could require a patent survey from the participant in conjunction with the submission of the service prototype to provide some evidence of novelty. Options are:

- Provided
- Not provided.

7.2   Contest Rules

Organisers often publish rules for their open digital innovation contests. The rules clarify important aspects of the contest including eligibility criteria, submission deadlines, evaluation criteria, prize and management of intellectual property. For example, the rules for the Olympic City Transport Challenge included "… contestant (s) retains ownership of all intellectual property rights in and to its intellectual property used and/or incorporated in the developed App., including documentation, submitted to the Challenge…" and "… companies or individuals with ties to the jury members are not eligible to participate". See Appendix for more examples of contest rules.

7.3   Budget

An open digital innovation contest is associated with costs, money as well as time and other resources. To give a straight answer to the question "How much does it cost to arrange an open digital innovation contest?" is not possible. The budget depends on a number of factors such as scope, length, number of participants and prize.

Table 7.4 Components of a typical budget for arranging open digital innovation contests

Budget component	Description
Contest design	Time for meetings and discussions
Marketing to attract participants	Cost and time for establishing a contest brand and profile, setting up a homepage and actively marketing the contest through different channels. Experience shows that this often requires a lot of individual contacts with potential participants
Platform and data	Cost and time for acquiring or developing a contest platform and to identify and make available data sources. Experience shows that there is a lot of work involved in establishing a useful set of data sources and APIs
Resources and facilitation	Cost and time for developing resources such as user personae, case descriptions and business model toolbox as well as cost and time for planning and arranging meetings (physical or digital) to facilitate participants, including costs for key-note speakers
Final event.	Cost and time for planning and arranging a final event, including costs for jury members, such as travelling and lodgings
Prize	Cost for arranging prizes
Post-contest support	Cost and time for providing support to participants after the contest is finished
Project management	Cost and time for managing the entire contest project

To arrange an open digital innovation contest of high quality that attracts good external developers and that will yield a reasonable output will require a budget of between fifty and one hundred thousand euros. A less ambitious event may, of course, cost less, while a large contest that spans several months and includes a number of meetings and a comprehensive IT platform will cost more. For example, the budget for the Electricity Challenge totalled one hundred and forty-six thousand euros where fifty-four thousand euros were provided by Vinnova and ninety-two thousand euros were provided in-kind by eighteen consortium partners.

The components of a typical budget are presented in Table 7.4.

7.4 Activities

The activity *Design Contest* aims at designing a contest format that has the best conditions to fulfil the contest goals, e.g. to improve public transport in a particular city. Typically, this activity would start in conjunction with discussing contest goals and budget with one or a few stakeholders. In conjunction with this activity and *Engage stakeholders*, the desired types of participants are identified. Based on these discussions the contest format is decided. Here Tables 7.1 and 7.2 provide guidance to the organisers. Once the format is decided, the details of the contest design are articulated by configuring the detailed design elements presented above. Some of the design elements are given by the chosen contest format while other design elements need to be configured to fit the specific conditions of the contest. Moreover, in conjunction with the activity *Develop Platform*, the needs and opportunities in terms of data sources and developers' platform are discussed. The budget for the chosen contest design is estimated and the prospective limitations of the budget are discussed and may lead to updates of the contest design.

7.4.1 Sub-activities

1. Assess contest goals and stakeholder goals
2. Choose contest format
3. Configure design elements to fit contest goals and chosen format
4. Develop contest rules based on the contest design
5. Establish contest budget.

7.5 Running Example

The Olympic City Transport Challenge aimed to improve public transport during and after the 2016 Rio Olympics. It was organised according to the Innovation Challenge format to result in a few services ready for implementation after the contest. The challenge was divided into three categories: Travel planner, Comfort and accessibility and Experience the Olympics. However, the target group was only specified for one of the three challenge categories, Travel Planner, although this category was considered as the most important and demanding one. In this category, participants had to show that their travel planner previously had been successfully used in other cities. The contest time period was long, five months, to give participants sufficient time to develop a solid service. The contest was divided into two phases: first, a conceptual phase and second, an implementation phase. The submissions were evaluated by a jury after each of the two phases. The prize consisted of the right of the winning participants to use the Olympic City brand to promote their services. For two of the categories there was also a monetary prize of up 3000 euros to travel to Rio. Table 7.5 presents the configuration of the design elements for the contest.

The contest design was communicated to the partners in a document called "Contest Brief". The contest brief was used by the organisers to establish the project plan as a baseline for marketing and communication and to estimate the budget for the contest.

Table 7.5 Example of the contest design from the Olympic City Transport Challenge

Design element	Selected option
1. Media, environment of innovation contest	Offline
2. Organiser, entity initiating innovation contest	Public organisations
3. Task/topic specificity, solution space of innovation contest	Defined in three different service categories
4. Degree of elaboration	Phase 1: Concept Phase 2: Solution
5. Target group, description of participants	Unspecified, however for one service category there were demands for past business experience
6. Participation as, number of people forming one entity of participant	Both individual and team
7. Contest period	Very long term
8. Reward/motivation	Non-monetary and monetary
9. Community functionality, platform functionalities for interaction between participants	Not given
10. Evaluation, method to determine ranking of submissions	Jury evaluation
11. User Needs	User category descriptions.
12. Business Value	Not available
13. Data	Open data and API
14. Innovation Novelty	Not available
15. Post-contest support, level of support provided to participants to implement service after the innovation contest had ended	B, as the resources (data and developers' platform) remained available to the winners

7.6 Guidelines

- Discuss the contest design and the design elements carefully and make informed choices. Once the contest design is finalised, most decisions on how to conduct the contest have been taken and they will be very difficult to change in later stages.
- Prioritise design elements to fit your particular conditions.

7.7 Read More

More information about design elements for digital innovation contests can be found in the articles written by Bullinger and Moeslein (2010), Hjalmarsson and Rudmark (2012) and Juell-Skielse et al. (2014).

References

Bullinger, A. C., & Moeslein, K. (2010). Innovation contests—Where are we? *Innovation, 8,* 1–2010.

Hjalmarsson, A., & Rudmark, D. (2012). Designing digital innovation contests. In K. Peters, M. Rothenberger, & B. Kuechler (Eds.), *Design science research in information systems. Advances in theory and practice* (Vol. 7286, pp. 9–27). Berlin: Springer.

Juell-Skielse, G., Hjalmarsson, A., Juell-Skielse, E., Johannesson, P., & Rudmark, D. (2014). Contests as innovation intermediaries in open data markets. *Information Polity, 19*(3,4), 247–262.

Mankins, J. (1995). Technology readiness levels. *A White Paper*, NASA, Washington, DC.

Chapter 8
Develop Contest Platform

Abstract This chapter explains how a contest platform can support different stakeholders, prior, during and after the contest. First, the notion of a contest platform is described. This is followed by a description of the activity, followed by running examples that guide the organizer to select and develop a suitable contest platform. *Develop contest platform* is affected by the contest design, but also affect which stakeholders to engage in the pre-contest phase. The notion of a platform has several meanings as we explore in the Read More section concluding this chapter.

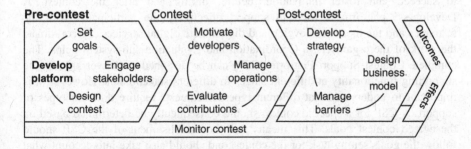

Develop contest platform is an activity in the pre-contest phase of the open digital innovation process. A contest platform is the digital support needed for organisers to prepare and run the contest and to offer the level of assistance that the organiser aims to provide after the contest. As Fig. 8.1 displays, a Contest Support Platform (CSP) is accessible not only to organisers but also to beneficiaries, participants and resource providers. It can include different sub-systems that provide means for communication, coordination, evaluation, software development and dissemination in the different phases of the contest.

Fig. 8.1 Contest support platform including main user types and sub-systems

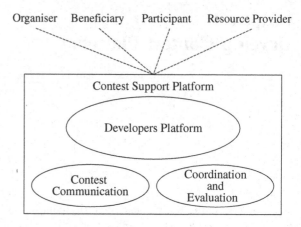

8.1 A Website Is not Good Enough

Organisers often only focus on establishing an information website to communicate about their contest. This communication is supported by the Contest Communication sub-system, see Fig. 8.1. However, this is often not enough to satisfy the needs of a contest. Additional types of IT support are normally required to succeed and foster innovation, before, during and after the contest. A Developers' platform is used to support effectively the participants with the resources and the means to develop and disseminate digital services. To coordinate the work of the organisers, a Coordination and Evaluation sub-system helps. The complete Contest Support Platform (CSP) can be designed to deliver appropriate supporting functionality at different stages to different stakeholders. However, it is important to understand that different types of contests require different types of support. A CSP for a specific contest should consequently be determined based on the agreed contest goals. This means that the establishment of the CSP should follow the goals setting task for the contest and should also take into account what the different types of stakeholders engaged.

8.1.1 Developers' Platform

Developers' Platform is a sub-system of the CSP. The platform offers a set of features that includes resources, the building blocks offered to participants to support innovation of service prototypes. These resources may include digitised domain knowledge describing the intended use context of the solutions, e.g. persona, vision and scenarios. Other examples of digital resources are open data provided through APIs, links to available open data resources external to the organisers, as well as operational use of these resources, e.g. written specifications, FAQs, virtual assistance and chatrooms.

A key idea for an open digital innovation contest is to develop service solutions. In order to simplify the distribution of these solutions to customers, users or stakeholders beyond the contest, a Developers' Platform can provide digital support both to display the outcome of the contest and to offer the service solutions to customers and end-users. It can include a leader board so that the positions can be seen during the contest and for the final result. It can also support dissemination of the results through a storefront to display service solutions, i.e. a potential market place to connect participants with e.g. venture capital, resource providers and end-users. The dissemination support could also include news, e.g. interviews with the winning teams, organisers and sponsors sharing information about the contributions, lessons learned and experiences from the contest.

The Developers' Platform could either be an extension of the Contest Communication sub-system or a stand-alone sub-system. In the first alternative, an extended Contest Communication sub-system not only provides information about the contest, but also provides resources that support the teams during the contest. This alternative is less costly but does not provide so much support for development. This is preferable for smaller and non-recurring contests. The second alternative, a stand-alone sub-system for extensive development support, is a rich and extensible foundation of digital resources that includes the necessary interfaces and APIs that make the digital resources more accessible to the developers. This alternative is preferable for larger and recurring contests closely connected to a developer community or a larger professional network of developers.

8.1.2 Contest Communication

Contest Communication is also a sub-system of the CSP, it provides support in the pre- and the contest phase, see Fig. 8.1. It is used to communicate information about the contest to stakeholders outside the boundaries of the organising team. Contest Communication provides an interface between the contest organisers and the different types of external stakeholders, such as potential participants, enrolled participants, resource providers, beneficiaries and followers interested in the contest. Information channelled through this sub-system is often related to the contest and the organisers, the challenges that the contest promotes, instructions for how to enrol as a participant, enrolment functionality, contest rules, prize information, events associated with the contest, news and details about the contest process. An illustrative example of a Contest Communication sub-system is the web-site for the contest, the ElectriCity Innovation Challenge 2015, see Fig. 8.2.

The web-site provided key features for communicating the challenge to external stakeholders, with a focus on potential and enrolled contest participants. It also provided interfaces to the innovation platform to trigger potential participants to enrol and enrolled participants to navigate challenges associated with participation. An extension to a Contest Communication sub-system is to connect it to social

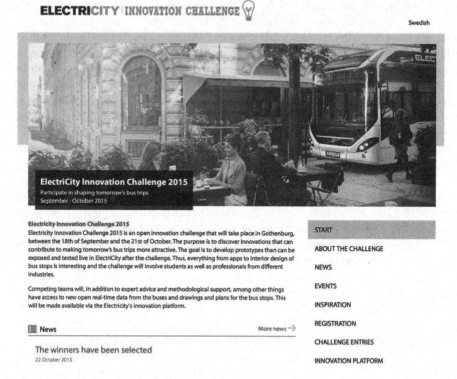

Fig. 8.2 The contest communication sub-system for the contest, the electricity innovation challenge 2015

media, such as Facebook and Twitter. This way organisers can more easily reach a wider and larger audience.

8.1.3   Coordination and Evaluation

Coordination and Evaluation provides project management support for the organisers. The main reason for the sub-system is to provide an internal shared infrastructure used to structure planning, contest design, operation and post-contest support as a project. That is to set and communicate goals between stakeholders, to define the format for the competition and to organise the contest and its aftermath as a process, i.e. activity structure and time scheduling. This sub-system also provides assistance to divide systematically labour between the organisers throughout the design process and also to organise the involvement of organisers when the contest is operational. During the contest operation, the sub-system is used to execute activities and to monitor and control progress, including identifying and resolving problems. Also, the sub-system provides support to assess the outcome of the contest, raise experiences and facilitate the communication of the results internally within the organising team. This sub-system may include standard software solutions for project management, such as Projectplace and Podio.

8.2   Activity Description

The activity, *Establish Contest Platform,* aims to ensure that an appropriate information system is implemented for the contest. The information system is likely to have sub-systems of different types. Some are more internal for the design and operation of the contest, as well as sub-systems that aim to provide external support to prospective and engaged participants. Typically, this activity would start with a review of the contest goals and use these as requirements to determine what sub-systems the CSP should include and their functionality. An important part of the activity is to identify what digital resources should be made available to the contestants and how. The activity uses the outcome from the activity *Set goals* and is performed in tandem with the activity Design contest so that the CSP adheres to the format chosen for the contest. The deployment of the sub-systems could imply that some functionality has to be developed, implemented or even procured if it is not readily available within the contest organisation. The activity is completed when the CSP is implemented and verified. However, as is common in the implementation of digital support, changes and improvements to the support infrastructure are likely to occur throughout the lifecycle of the contest to meet new support needs.

8.2.1   Sub-activities

1. Define requirements based on contest goals, stakeholder needs, contest design and available time-frame and budget.
2. Develop a satisfactory Contest Support Platform through:

   a. Selection and adaptation of packaged software
   b. Additional in-house development.

3. Test and validate the Contest Support Platform and its dependent sub-systems.
4. Launch the Contest Support Platform and its dependent sub-systems to the users based on a carefully developed deployment plan.

8.3   Running Examples

In the case of the ElectriCity Innovation Challenge 2015, the Control and Evaluation sub-system consisted of a proprietary off-the-shelf software for project management that was made available to the contest project by one of the organisers. All contest design and internal contest coordination were channelled through this software. The nineteen organisations involved in organising the contest were connected to this software solution and used it as a shared support infrastructure to manage the contest process. In a similar way, the Volvo Car Challenge 2013 also used an off-the-shelf software to design and coordinate the contest. In TravelHack 2013, the contest organisation, in this case three organisers and one contest consultancy company, used the Google Apps for Work service to manage the contest process. In all of these cases, the selection of the Developers' Platform sub-system was based on (1) need for support functionality (2) financial resources for the project and (3) the availability of present sub-systems within the control of the organisers.

TravelHack 2013 and the ElectriCity Innovation Challenge 2015 developed original Contest Communication sub-systems to communicate the contest to stakeholders. The main reasons for developing original sub-systems were that (1) no existing infrastructure could be re-used or adapted and (2) the contest format was inclusive, meaning that the open innovation process was open for everyone to participate. The Volvo Car Challenge 2015 was closed, only including organisational members in the Vehicle ICT Arena in Sweden. Instead, the Contest Communication sub-system was developed as an integrated part of the website for the arena. With a more specific target group of participants, less functionality and content was needed for this sub-system compared to the Contest Communication sub-system provided for TravelHack and the ElectriCity Innovation Challenge respectively. The Contest Communication sub-systems communicated the challenges that each contest promoted, specifications describing how potential contestants could enrol, enrolment functionality, contest rules, information about the prizes, planned events associated with the contest, news and the contest process.

The TravelHack 2013 Contest Communication sub-system provided links (1) to the Developers' Platform promoted by the contest organisers (Trafiklab) as well as (2) to external open data resources associated with the contest (based on their relevance to the three contest challenges) and (3) to other digitised resources with relevance to the contestants. The Developers' Platform promoted by TravelHack 2013 had been developed two years prior to the contest and contained open data and services connected to public transport in Sweden. The Developers' Platform for the ElectriCity Innovation Challenge 2015 was developed for that contest. It included, in addition to open data from the electrified public transport, other digitised resources relevant to the contest, such as personae and blueprints over bus stops. Similarly to TravelHack 2013, the Contest Communication sub-system EIC 2015 provided links to the Developers' Platform and further digitised resources for the teams. The Developers' Platform in the Volvo Car Challenge was decoupled from the Contest Communication sub-system. It consisted of a simulator to be used by the teams to build their prototypes and to provide a visual contribution to the expert jury.

For outcome dissemination, Travelhack 2013 used the Developers' Platform for the contest—TrafikLab.se. All contributing teams presented their contribution on that part of the platform which gave free access to the public. Consequently, the Developers' Platform was used both as the mechanism to distribute resources for the teams to develop their prototypes and as the shared infrastructure to present their results. As Travelhack 2013 aimed to develop prototypes for mobile applications that enhanced the use of public transportfor citizens, the final digital service was not published on TrafikLab.se; instead these were published on the Nordic App. Store and Google Play. In the ElectriCity Innovation-Challenge 2015, the contributions from the contest were published using the Contest Communication sub-system. The contributions were presented with films that both illustrated the concept idea and the final prototype. Due to intellectual property restrictions, the Volvo Car Challenges had no specific sub-system for presenting and disseminating the contributions from the contest. Via the Vehicle ICT Arena website, the three final teams were presented with brief descriptions of their final contributions.

8.4 Read More

Platform as a concept has been researched for a long time in the fields of management and information systems. Tiwana (2013) defined a software platform as a software-based product or service that functions as a base on which outside parties can build complementary products or services. He argues that a software platform is an extensible software-based system that provides core functionality shared by applications that interoperate with it and the interfaces through which they interoperate (c.f. Baldwin and Woodard 2009; Tiwana et al. 2010). In this chapter, when we talk about a Contest Support Platform with sub-systems, the sub-system Developers' Platform resembles what Tiwana (2013) describes as the software platform. In other words, open digital innovation contests aim to structure the process through which the capacity provided by the Developers' Platform is used by participants. Compared to traditional software development, open digital innovation, driven by a contest approach, uses platforms to take advantage of the expertise of a targeted developer community, to develop digital services that adhere to defined overall goals (Hjalmarsson and Rudmark 2012). The use of platforms means that the locus of innovation can be relocated from the organisation to the massive network of developers available outside the realms of the specific organisation, via either outside-in innovation, inside-out innovation or coupled innovation (Gassmann and Enkel 2004).

References

Baldwin, C., & Woodard, J. (2009). The architecture of platforms: A unified view. In A. Gawer (Ed.), *Platforms, markets and innovation*. Cheltenham, UK: Edward Elgar.

Gassmann, O., & Enkel, E. (2004). Towards a theory of open innovation: Three core process archetypes. Proceedings of *The R&D Management Conference*. Lisbon, Portugal, July 6–9.

Hjalmarsson, A., & Rudmark, D. (2012). Designing digital innovation contests. In K. Peffers, M. Rothenberger & Kuechler (Eds.), *DESRIST 2012, LNCS 7286* (pp 9–27).

Tiwana, A. (2013). *Platform ecosystems: Aligning architecture, governance and strategy*. Waltman, MA: Morgan Kaufman.

Tiwana, A., Konsynski, B., & Bush, A. (2010). Platform evolution: Coevolution of architecture, governance, and environmental dynamics. *Information System Research, 21*(4), 675–687.

Chapter 9
Motivate Developers

Abstract In this chapter, we present motivational factors for external developers and discuss how to motivate different types of contest participants. The activity *Motivate developers* is presented in conjunction with a running example. The chapter ends with a suggestion for further reading.

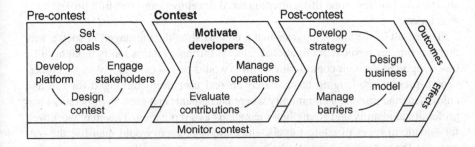

Participants in open digital innovation contests are normally not paid for the effort they make. Instead, they engage in the development of ideas and services for other reasons, e.g., the opportunity to win a prize. But research has found that contest participants engage freely for many different reasons, such as the sheer joy of programming or the opportunity to learn a new technical platform.

A distinction can be made between intrinsic and extrinsic motivation. Intrinsic motivation is when you engage in a behaviour because you experience personal satisfaction. You do something for its own sake. In contrast, extrinsic motivation is when you do something in order to be rewarded or to avoid punishment. The main difference is that intrinsic motivation comes from within the individual, while extrinsic motivation arises from outside the individual.

In Chap. 6, participants are divided into five categories: citizens, community developers, students, entrepreneurial developers and professional developers. Citizens and community developers are primarily motivated by intrinsic factors such as fun and the intellectual challenge of solving societal needs. Students, as

© Springer International Publishing AG 2017

A. Hjalmarsson et al., *Open Digital Innovation*, Progress in IS,

DOI 10.1007/978-3-319-56339-8_9

well as entrepreneurial and professional developers, are primarily motivated by extrinsic factors like money, business relationships and skills development.

Depending on the innovation problem at hand, different categories of participants are best suited to solve the problem. If the innovation problem requires cumulative knowledge and new solutions are developed based on past advances, then community developers and citizens are preferred. In this situation, intrinsic motivational factors become more important. But, if the innovation problem is better solved through experimentation using several technical approaches and involving numerous customer groups, then entrepreneurial and professional developers, as well as students, are favoured. In this case extrinsic motivational factors are more important.

In a study of motivational factors for participants in open digital innovation contests, it was found that intrinsic motivation was most important, see Table 9.1. The top three factors were fun and enjoyment, intellectual challenge and status and reputation. User need, an extrinsic type of motivation, scores fairly high while other extrinsic factors score the lowest, including money, reciprocity and signalling and career concerns. The participants consisted of teams representing different categories, where two fifths viewed themselves as community developers, one fifth students and citizens, one fifth entrepreneurial developers and one fifth professional developers.

The result of the study suggests that a contest should be arranged in such a way that it promotes intrinsic motivational factors. Intrinsic motivation is thought to be best supported through communities. But it would be too easy to say that a contest should present challenging tasks, based on real user needs, arranged for fun and enjoyment and provide a community where participants can grow their personal and professional identity and strengthen their status and reputation. This may work well for outside-in types of contest goals, since the organisers would then use the outcome of the contest as input to their own innovation. But, if the contest also has inside-out and coupled goals, where the participants are expected to continue innovation, then intrinsic motivation has to be balanced with extrinsic motivation.

Table 9.1 The importance of motivational factors for participation in open digital innovation contests. 7 is the highest and 1 the lowest possible score (Juell-Skielse et al. 2014, p. 284)

Motivation	Avg.	Dev.	Type
Fun and enjoyment	6.8	0.6	Intrinsic
Intellectual challenge	6.3	1.2	Intrinsic
Status and reputation	6.0	1.4	Intrinsic
User need	5.8	1.6	Extrinsic
Professional and personal identity	5.5	1.8	Intrinsic
Autonomy	5.3	1.8	Intrinsic
Learning and skills development	4.9	2.0	Extrinsic
Money	4.9	1.8	Extrinsic
Reciprocity	4.7	1.9	Both
Signalling and career concerns	4.3	2.2	Extrinsic

Extrinsic motivation is thought to be favoured by market mechanisms. Therefore, it goes without saying that, if external developers are expected to continue innovation and to commercialise their service prototypes or engage in coupled innovation, the business terms and conditions must be clear in order to decrease their risks. It would be naïve for organisers to expect a contest to result in services commercialised by the participants, without providing extrinsic motivation and market mechanisms for service implementation and operation.

9.1   Motivating Different Types of Participants

Based on experiences from a number of contests, it has been found that different types of external developers are motivated in different ways, see Table 9.2. The main motives for citizen developers seem to be that they want to contribute to society by solving a problem or a challenge in the use domain. Also, intrinsic motives such as fun and enjoyment seem to be important.

Community developers often have a strong interest in the open digital resources provided by the contest. That is, what can be done with the data sets, and how these data sets can be used to improve available solutions. In order to attract this developer type, the organisers need to emphasise the digital resources made available by the contest. Novel data sources, not previously provided, can

Table 9.2 Motivational factors for different types of participants

Sub-type	Key motives for participation
Citizen	– Mainly intrinsic and non-commercial motives – Solving a challenge experienced by the team where the solution can be of benefit to others – Interested to contribute to the solution of a societal problem
Community developer	– Mainly intrinsic and non-commercial motives – Explore the value and possibilities of digital resources – Have fun
Student	– Achieve course and learning goals – Market the student towards future employers – Intellectual challenge
Entrepreneurial developer	– Encourage the pursuit of a joint entrepreneurial endeavour – Push idea to prototype or enhanced prototype – Use contest prize to formalise organisational setting – Develop business relationships
Professional developer	– Create or strengthen business relationship – Explore new business opportunity – Team building – Capability building – Improve company brand

encourage participation. Also, peer-based engagement can be used to mobilise interest in the contest. In other words, if some developers who are regarded as highly capable are attracted to the contest, then their peers within the community are likely to join.

Students are often motivated by non-commercial motives. They are driven also by objectives connected to their studies. Attracting students on a large-scale normally requires that contest participation is strongly linked to an academic course.

There is a difference in motivation between, on the one hand, citizens, community developers and students and, on the other hand, entrepreneurial and professional developers. The former are seldom driven by commercial interests. Also, if they win and there are commercial rewards, it will not automatically mean that non-commercial motives are replaced by commercial interests to deploy the solution. One explanation is that these kinds of developer do not have the mind-set to transform their solution into a business. Another explanation is that they lack the capabilities to transform a non-commercial practice into a commercially driven process. This must be taken into account when the contest is designed, see Chap. 7, as well as when the level of support in the post-process is decided, see Chap. 12.

Entrepreneurial developers often participate in a contest because it provides a mechanism to build business relationships with potential client and partner organisations. Entrepreneurial developers are often attracted by a contest prize that will help them to form or strengthen a start-up business. Moreover, a contest offers an opportunity to push a service idea to a prototype or to improve an existing prototype by integrating it with additional digital resources.

Professional developers are often motivated by the opportunity to strengthen business relationships with the contest organisers. The reason could be to explore a new business opportunity or to develop a solution that can be sold to the problem owner. Another reason could be to demonstrate the capabilities of the organisation that the professional developer represents. Moreover, the contest could be an opportunity to explore a new business idea. Then the contest offers a systematic process to transform the idea to a digital service prototype, which is also evaluated by a jury. Additional motives are that contest participation strengthens the capability within the professional developer's organisation as well as its corporate brand.

9.2 Activity Description

The activity *Motivate developers* aims at stimulating participants to submit contributions that correspond to the organisers' innovation goals. The activity starts by understanding the characteristics of the participants that the organisers aim to attract to the contest. Based on these characteristics, motivational factors are identified and means are developed to match them.

9.2.1 Sub-activities

1. Understand developers' characteristics
2. Identify motivational factors
3. Develop means to stimulate motivational factors.

9.3 Running Example

In the Olympic City Transport Challenge, the aim was to make Rio de Janeiro's public transport and urban mobility more reliable, comfortable and accessible. One of the contest categories was Travel Planner. In this category, the goal was to make transport data openly available for external developers to create apps. that supported users in advanced trip planning during the Olympics. The apps. should also have led to lasting improvements that remained after the games were finished. Three user categories were identified: regular users, visitors to the Olympics and occasional users.

The type of innovation in this contest category was inside-out, where open data produced by the city of Rio de Janeiro were exploited by external developers. The innovation problem was characterised by adapting different technical solutions to the needs of the different user categories in the context of Rio de Janeiro. The contest winner was expected to offer a viable business model of the travel planner. Also, it was a requirement that the participant had experience of operating the travel planner in other large cities.

This is an example of a digital innovation contest where the organisers wanted to attract professional developers who were able to provide apps. to a large number of end users in a competitive market. The motivational factors were primarily extrinsic and the main means to stimulate professional developers to participate was a prize that helped them in marketing their travel planner. The prize consisted of the exclusive right to use the "Olympic City" brand, owned by the City of Rio de Janeiro, when promoting the app.

9.4 Read More

This chapter is primarily based on two articles investigating open innovation, motivational factors and digital innovation contests. Boudreau and Lakhani (2009) present a motivation model for how to manage outside innovation. They discuss the differences between organising open innovation as communities of practice and as competitive markets. They argue that communities of practice are better motivated through intrinsic factors while competitive markets are driven by extrinsic factors. They also present a number of intrinsic and extrinsic motivational factors relevant to open innovation. Juell-Skielse et al. (2014) studied motivational factors for participating in open digital innovation contests. They applied the model presented by Boudreau and Lakhani (2009) and measured the importance of the motivational factors as perceived by participants in two open digital innovation contests. The result is presented in Table 9.1. They concluded that intrinsic factors are the most important to motivate external developers to participate in open digital innovation contests.

References

Boudreau, K. J., & Lakhani, K. R. (2009). How to manage outside innovation. *MIT Sloan Management Review, 50*(4), 69–75.
Juell-Skielse, G., Hjalmarsson, A., Johannesson, P., & Rudmark, D. (2014, September). Is the public motivated to engage in open data innovation? Proceedings of *International Conference on Electronic Government* (pp. 277–288). Berlin Heidelberg. Springer.

Chapter 10
Manage Contest Operations

Abstract This chapter provides a description of how to manage contest operations. It starts by presenting common problems encountered during contest operations. Then proactive and reactive measures to deal with these problems are suggested. The activity *Manage operations* is described in sub-activities and followed by guidelines. The chapter concludes with several examples.

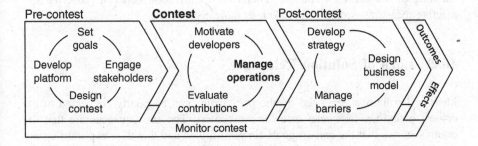

Manage Contest Operations is the second activity in the contest phase. It is influenced by project management and highlights the need for planning, executing, monitoring and controlling contest operations. The approach in this book accentuates the need to prepare key activities prior to the contest, in order to be able to operate it successfully as an open innovation process. Despite the emphasis on preparing these activities, preparations will not be enough to ensure the success of the contest.

A well prepared contest enables the organising team to manage proactively different problems that will occur throughout its operations. One key characteristic of open digital innovation is that the organising team actively attracts external developers to participate. This participation is often funded and organised by the external developers themselves. It means that the organisers have limited or no control over the engagement that the developers put into the innovation process when it has begun. Depending on established agreements, this is often also the case with resource providers. Instead, the organisers have to work proactively to meet the expectations that different stakeholders have of the contest process, both to retain them in the contest and to stimulate them to generate useful results.

10.1   Common Problems Encountered in Contest Operations

There are a number of common problems that can occur during the operation of a contest. In this section, six common problems, based on experiences from a number of contests, are presented, see Table 10.1. Their consequences are discussed together with suggestions for proactive and reactive measures for problem management.

Proactive measures are implemented before problems occur while reactive measures are taken when problems have occurred. Some of the suggested measures are applicable to more than one problem. For example, direct communication with participants through facilitation and ideas check-up seminars is a measure used to manage several of the problems. Some measures can be taken both proactively and reactively. For example, facilitation and ideas check-up seminars could be scheduled in advance and also be used reactively to strengthen participants' understanding of a contest's challenge. Therefore, the division between proactive and reactive measures is only to be taken as indicative.

10.2   Lack of Solution Relevance

Ideas and solutions generated by the participants can be poorly connected to the contest goals, i.e. lack relevance for the contest. The consequences are that the organisers risk that the contest goals are not fulfilled and that their expectations are not met. However, there are several proactive and reactive measures which can be used to manage this problem, see Table 10.2.

10.3   Lack of Innovation

Sometimes the ideas and solutions produced during a contest fail to be innovative. The consequences are that the organisers have little use for the output in their own innovation processes and also that participants risk losing interest in the contest and

Table 10.1 Common problems to contest operations	Problem
	• Lack of goal fulfilment and solution relevance • Lack of innovation • Lack of team performance • Lack of resources • Inadequate use of available resources • Ineffective communication

Table 10.2 Suggested measures to manage lack of goal fulfilment

Proactive measures	Reactive measures
• Define appropriate contest challenges. Provide digital resources (e.g. personae, use cases) that enable the teams to scope their ideas to adhere to the contest goals • Ensure that the platform provides easy access to stimulating digital resources • Adapt and adopt a method of monitoring team participation, engagement and progress • Define and use a transparent procedure for contribution, evaluation and communication of results	• Perform facilitation and ideas check-up seminars • Lower threshold for participants to use digital resources and, if possible, add new digital resources to the platform • Provide feedback to individual teams on the quality and value of their achievement

Table 10.3 Suggested measures to manage lack of innovation

Proactive measures	Reactive measures
• Provide resources (e.g. a vision, user persona, a review of existing services, use cases) that stimulate teams' innovation • Design and schedule activities to inspire and coach participants, e.g. meetings with problem owner and end-users • Stimulate appropriate staffing for the teams • Provide a review of digital services available on the market • Ensure that the platform provides easy access to stimulating digital resources • Plan for and prepare contest organisers and resource providers to engage with teams about ideas if needed	• Conduct ideas check-ups where teams are challenged to present the output from the ideas phase and receive feedback • Monitor team progress and provide a communication channel to discuss barriers and provide facilitation • Perform facilitation and ideas check-up seminars • Lower threshold for participants to use digital resources and, if possible, add new digital resources to the platform

prioritising other activities. Suggestions for proactive and reactive measures to cope with this problem are presented in Table 10.3.

10.4 Lack of Team Performance

Participants can underperform, for example, due to a lack of competence or a lack of time for innovation. The consequences are that the quality of the output does not meet the contest goals. Also that participants are unable to transform their ideas into innovative and solid prototypes. Moreover, it can happen that participants fail to submit their solutions for the final evaluation. Suggestions for measures to cope with this problem are presented in Table 10.4.

Table 10.4 Suggested measures to manage lack of team performance

Proactive measures	Reactive measures
• Design a contest that provides both a rigorous process and facilitates the development of relevant solutions • Advertise early the expected competence requirements to complete the challenge • Plan for and prepare contest organisers and resource providers to engage with teams in prototype development, if needed • Use the platform to monitor team progress and ambitions • Ensure that the platform has functionality to communicate immediate feedback to teams	• Allow the teams to add competences to the team up to a pre-defined cap • Monitor team progress and coach teams to manage development barriers • Provide feedback to individual teams on the quality and value of their achievement • Communicate feedback to teams via the platform regarding the capacity of resources provided • Add requested digital resources if possible

10.5   Lack of Resources

There could be a lack of resources. For example, there could a lack of quality in the provided resources or essential building blocks could be missing. Also there could be a lack of operational resources necessary to operate the contest or to fund the prizes. The consequences are that participants develop solutions that do not meet the evaluation criteria or that specific stages in the contest-driven approach cannot be delivered with appropriate quality. Moreover, external developers could be unable to transform ideas into working prototypes or the contest does not become attractive due to a lack of prizes. Suggestions for proactive and reactive measures to cope with this problem are presented in Table 10.5.

Table 10.5 Suggested measures to manage lack of resources

Proactive measures	Reactive measures
• Design an appropriate budget and allocate resources to match the costs in the budget, including the cost of prizes • Monitor actively the teams' progress and have available operational resources ready to add building blocks to the external developers • Assess the quality of the digital resources before they are made available to participant • Develop scenarios prior to the contest about addressing ideas on resources that are likely to be used by developers and add such resources to the contest	• Add sponsors that can provide additional funding to the contest • Add building blocks to the external developers • Re-plan the budget • Perform facilitation and ideas check-up seminars

Table 10.6 Suggested measures to manage inadequate use of available resources

Proactive measures	Reactive measures
• Promote contest resources to participants prior to the contest • Promote contest resources actively • Promote the contest actively via appropriate channels (e.g. social media) to attract relevant developers to the contest using the platform as a key component in the promotion campaign • Prepare one or several procedure(s) to access digital resources provided via the platform • Provide appropriate documentation regarding the content in the platform, create a channel (e.g. contest forum) for developers to ask questions and receive answers regarding the platform	• Promote contest resources to participants during the contest • Use communication channels to direct attention to provided resources. Provide facilitation for how to use resources • Promote the platform actively after the launch of the contest • Identify problems to access resources via the platform for service design and navigate barriers • Monitor questions from teams during the phase and provide answers via the platform

10.6   Inadequate Use of Available Resources

Digital resources that are available to the participants may not be properly used. There are several reasons for this, such as the participants not knowing about the resources or not understanding the capability of the platform. The consequences are that relevant external developers may not be attracted to the contest, that participants develop solutions that do not meet the evaluation criteria and that scarce resources are underused. Ultimately this could mean that the output does not adhere to the contest goals. Suggestions for proactive and reactive measures are presented in Table 10.6.

10.7   Ineffective Communication

Communication between the organisers and the participants can be ineffective. For example, organisers can fail to describe the contest challenges clearly or do not specify the rules or the reward. Participants can present their contributions poorly or forget to use the platform as the single point of contact with the organisers. The consequences are that participants may restrain their innovation capability and develop solutions that do not meet the contest goals. Also they underuse scarce digital resources and may lose interest in the contest and prioritise other activities. Moreover, if the participants do not use the platform as the main point of contact, the organisers may miss important messages and the contributions may be presented poorly which could make it difficult for the organisers to evaluate them. Suggestions for proactive and reactive measures to cope with this problem are presented in Table 10.7.

Table 10.7 Suggested measures to manage ineffective communication

Proactive measure	Reactive measure
• Develop a clear contest description • Design rewards adapted to participant types • Define and communicate transparent rules about output ownership and intellectual property • Ensure that the contest platform has the functionality required to absorb queries from participants and communicate answers that reach the contest community • Develop a systematic and prepared plan for presentation of contributions • Ensure that the platform has a contribution gallery that shows the contest results in a way that is promised to the participants	• Communicate contest challenge • Adjust contest prize • Collect questions by participants systematically and provide uniform answers to all participants • Market the platform as the main-point-of-contact for queries during the contest • Use buffer time to ensure a fair presentation and an evaluation of the contributions

10.8 Other Problems

In addition to the above problems, organisers can face other problems, such as the number of participants becoming less than expected and that simultaneous contests compete for the attention of the participants. A list of other problems and suggestions for measures to cope with them are presented in Table 10.8.

10.9 Activity Description

The activity *Manage Contest Operations*, aims to support the organising team to identify different problems that will hamper the contest. The organisers should continually monitor the progress of the contest operations using the evaluation approach adopted for the contest, see Chap. 15, and the contest design developed prior to the contest launch. They should watch for problems and triggers of present or future challenges and communicate to the appropriate responsible people any need to change plans, schedules, budgets or resources to reach the contest objectives. The organising team should also monitor these problems to be sure that they have been received, understood, acted upon and that they generate proper management actions. We divide the activity into two types of contest operation management, proactive and reactive, with attached sub-activities:

Table 10.8 Suggested measures to manage other problems in contest operations

Problem	Consequence	Proactive measure	Reactive measure
• The number of enrolled teams are below expectations	• The contest output does not match the contest objectives	• Develop and operate a recruitment plan to engage participants • Attract qualified participants based on appropriate incentives	• Monitor participation interest and adapt offer and incentives to participate depending on interest
• The number of teams engaged in the contest drops	• The contest does not match the organisers' expectations • The participants prioritise other engagements	• Adopt and adapt a method to monitor team participation and engagement	• Use ideas check-up seminars to retain engagement and problem participation
• The number of interested teams exceeds expectations	• The open digital innovation contest driven by the contest becomes too complex to operate	• Specify a limit to the number of possible participants, develop a set of transparent criteria to single out participants	• Re-plan and re-distribute contest resources
• Concurrent contests	• Developers prioritise other open digital innovation contests	• Plan the contest dates in relation to other concurrent contests	• Conduct interventions such as meetings to activate participants and increase engagement in the contest
• Non-transparent ranking of contributions	• Contest ranking is viewed as unfair by participants	• Develop clear criteria for evaluating contributions. Provide individual feedback to teams	• Prepare a common strategy to answer questions regarding the ranking

10.9.1   Sub-activities

1. Identify potential problems during contest planning.
2. Develop proactive measures, informed by Tables 10.2, 10.3, 10.4, 10.5, 10.6, 10.7, 10.8.
3. Monitor contest progress, implementing a contest measurement model, see Chap. 15.
4. Identify problems and develop reactive measures, informed by Tables 10.2, 10.3, 10.4, 10.5, 10.6, 10.7, 10.8.

10.10   Guidelines

The activity described in this section is based on an approach where the organising team proactively removes issues that are expected to cause problems in the contest and reactively identifies problems to act on during the contest. Therefore, it is recommended that the contest operation management is a recurrent activity that starts before the launch of the contest and continues to contest closure. We consequently recommend that the organising team, by using an adopted assessment model (see Chap. 15), reviews the progress of the contest and uses this input to change the course of actions that have caused or will cause problems in running the contest.

10.10.1   Guidelines

- Complement the assessment model with informal channels to investigate team performance and solution development, for example, by organising team leader meetings or simply through direct contact.
- Evaluate platform effectiveness through interviews and stimulate participants to suggest improvements, e.g. by setting up a virtual suggestion inbox.

10.11   Running Examples

Two examples of proactive management of problems during TravelHack 2013 were as follows. In order to stimulate the developers to create solutions that adhered to the challenges that the problem owners singled out to be solved, rough challenge descriptions were developed in parallel to set the problem goals. These descriptions were then tested on developers to understand how they perceived the challenges. This feedback was then used to change the descriptions. A professional communicator edited wording and scope before the challenges were presented to the developers. Another example of proactive management from Travelhack 2013 is connected to the challenge that good ideas are developed, however with a lack of innovation. To prevent this, Travelhack 2013 was split into one distinct ideas phase and one distinct service design phase. In the interface between these phases ideas were reviewed and twenty-four finalists were singled out from the sixty submissions received. The purpose with the split was to prevent non-innovative ideas from being transformed into services.

Two examples on reactive measures are taken from the ElectriCity Innovation Challenge 2015 and the Volvo Truck Open Challenge 2015. In the ElectriCity Innovation Challenge 2015, a digital forum was used to collect feedback from the sixty-five participating teams during the contest. The digital forum was an integrated part of the contest platform. The purpose with the digital forum was to collect issues that the teams faced during the contest, e.g. issues related to the provided open digital resources. One issue that surfaced from several of the groups was related to the description of one of the APIs. The developers did not understand some of the signals that were channelled through the API. The feedback enabled the organising teams to generate an updated description of the API. During the final of the Volvo Truck Open Challenge, the participating teams did individual presentations of their solutions to an expert jury. The presentations were approximately thirty minutes long and the schedule was tight. The problem that occurred was that the preparation work between the presentations took more time than predicted. The problem came to threaten the time schedule. In order to cope with the problem, the expert jury shifted between two rooms. When one team presented in one room, the next team prepared the presentation in a parallel room. This re-organisation solved the presentation issue and the time schedule was saved.

Chapter 11
Evaluate Contest Contributions

Abstract In this chapter, six methods for evaluating contest contributions are presented. The methods are described in terms of meaning and their implications on the presentation and submission of contributions. The methods are also mapped to the types of contest goals introduced in the activity *Set goals*, thereby providing guidance for choosing an evaluation method based on the contest goals. The chapter also contains a roadmap for choosing and preparing an evaluation method, as well as guidance as to how organisers should communicate evaluation results to the participants. The chapter is concluded with a running example section that describes experiences and lessons learned from several of the contests referred to in this book.

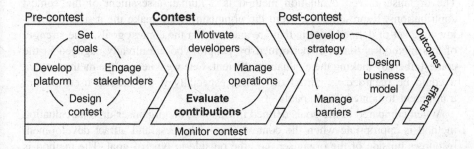

In order to evaluate the contributions from a contest, there are five basic methods that can be used to structure the assessment, see Table 11.1. The sixth method involves a combination of two or several of the basic evaluation methods. Besides a characterisation of the six methods, the table also includes a mapping between evaluation methods and contest goals. This mapping is not absolute, but it provides an indication for choosing an evaluation method based on the contest goal.

© Springer International Publishing AG 2017
A. Hjalmarsson et al., *Open Digital Innovation*, Progress in IS,
DOI 10.1007/978-3-319-56339-8_11

Table 11.1 Six methods for evaluating contest contributions

Evaluation method	Description	Suitability in relation to contest objectives			
		Outside-in	Inside-out	Coupled	Non-innovation
Organiser	Criteria-based human evaluation by contest organisers	X			X
Automated	Criteria-based machine evaluation by contest organisers	X	X		
Expert jury	Criteria-based human evaluation by expert jury	X	X		
Peer review	Guided human evaluation by fellow developer peers		X		X
Crowd source	Guided human evaluation by e.g. target users or public		X		X
Mixed	Evaluation through mixing evaluation methods		X	X	

11.1   The Organiser-Driven Evaluation Method

The organiser-driven evaluation method is a human assessment of the contest contributions. Representatives from the organising team make the assessment following a set of defined criteria that are anchored in the contest goals. One strength of this method is that it is performed by people who are already engaged in the contest, thereby making the evaluation efficient. One weakness of the method is that it could be regarded as partial or biased, especially if the criteria used are not transparent to contest participants.

When compared to the goals defined in Chap. 5, the organiser-driven evaluation method is appropriate when the contest aims to harness and attract development resources outside of the organiser, i.e., the outside-in type of goal. The method is also appropriate if the goal of the contest is not directly related to innovation, but instead to boosting the organiser's brand or to foster marketing.

11.2   The Automated Evaluation Method

The automated evaluation method is a machine-performed evaluation of the contest contributions. In this case, the evaluation procedure is automated and also governed by the organiser. Contributions are submitted in the form of executable prototypes (not ideas) and they are made available through scripts or a manual upload via the contest support platform. Submissions may or may not be scored immediately based on their efficiency relative to a pre-defined solution. The results can also be summarised on a results board. A strength, of the method is that it enables an efficient evaluation process together with a rigid assessment as well as live result boards. One example of this evaluation method is the contest platform Kaggle that uses automated evaluation for predictive modelling. Problem owners can post their data and challenges for external developers all over the world, who compete to produce the best solutions.

One challenge of this method is that it may require extensive preparation, as the automated evaluation procedure must be adapted for the contest challenge at hand. Another weakness is that automated evaluation requires a non-open contest challenge to facilitate benchmark and comparison and also that the contribution developed is executable. Consequently, solidity is assessed rather than the level of innovation in the solution. It could also, similarly to the organiser-driven evaluation method, be regarded as partial if the criteria used are not transparent to the contest participants.

When compared to the goals defined in Chap. 5, the automated evaluation method is appropriate when the competition aims to attract development resources outside the organiser to address a specific and restricted challenge. It is also suitable for use when the contest aims to solve challenges involving prediction and data mining by providing large amounts of data as open digital resources.

11.3 The Expert Jury Evaluation Method

The expert jury evaluation method is similar to the organiser-method, as it is a human based approach to assess the contest contributions. It is also based on a set of criteria used to distinguish the winner from all the submitted contributions. The criteria should be anchored in the contest goals and they will be used by the jury members to assess and rank the digital prototypes during or before the contest final. The difference between this method and the organiser-driven method is that the assessment group has been expanded with representatives from beneficiaries who are not among the organisers. These could include representatives from resource providers, potential solution funders, academia or other organisations that possess expert knowledge about the theme of the contest.

A strength of the method is that the judging team is broadened beyond the contest organisers, thereby combatting partiality and bias. Another strength is that the jury is staffed with individuals who have expert knowledge and experiences relevant to the contest theme, the criteria used or the solutions that have been developed. This empowers the jury, enabling a multi-viewed evaluation of the solutions. One challenge for the method is the recruitment of suitable jury members. Another issue is the calibration of the evaluation criteria, i.e. to ensure that all jury members interpret them in the same way. Yet another challenge to overcome is related to transferring knowledge about the different solutions to the jury members. An expert jury group will not be able to follow the competition as closely as the organisers. Experiences from Travelhack 2011 show that an expert jury has only a limited time to understand the solutions, especially with regard to user value and market potential.

When compared to the goals defined in Chap. 5, the expert-jury evaluation method is appropriate when the contest aims to harness and attract development resources outside of the organiser, i.e., the outside-in type of goal. It is also suitable to adopt when the contest aims to solve vague and complex challenges, which makes automated evaluation hard or impossible.

11.4 The Peer-Review Evaluation Method

In the peer-review method, the participants in the contest are also the evaluators of the contributions. When the contest ends, the participants present their solutions to each other. Using a guiding procedure for rating submissions, the participants are then tasked to rank the contributions in order to identify the winner or winners.

A strength of the peer-review method is that it has high confidence among participants, especially if the developers are community and idealistically driven. The peer-review becomes a mechanism through which the community is strengthened as the contest dimension is downplayed. A challenge of the method is that the organisers' control of the evaluation process is weaker than in the previous methods. The control of judging results and rewarding decisions is decentralised to the participants, who might interpret contest goals and evaluation guidance differently from that which the organisers intended. This may be not be a problem if the contest goal is non-innovative or if the contest is organised with an inside-out aim to increase the interest for the open data. However, if the aim is to outside-in harness creativity beyond organisational boundaries, then decentralisation of the judging power might come into conflict with the organisers' goals.

11.5 The Crowd-Sourcing Evaluation Method

An even more decentralised approach than the peer-review method, is the crowd-sourcing method. When applying this method, the participants make their contributions available to stakeholders outside the contest for final review. The crowd, e.g. targeted users or the public, is then invited to assess and place votes on the contributions following a pre-defined guide for evaluation.

A strength of this method is that it enables the organisers to determine the contest outcome based on the "customer voice" about the solutions. At the same time it mobilises an interest for the contest and its outcomes beyond the participating stakeholders. One challenge is how to transfer knowledge about the solutions to the crowd. In Travelhack 2014, this issue was resolved through a virtual gallery on the contest support platform where each solution was presented with a text that followed a structured template, screen shots of the prototype and a one-minute film pitching the service. The contest support platform also included a voting mechanism through which the public could vote for their favourite. Two additional challenges of this method are the difficulties of reaching out to the crowd and the time-consumption of the voting procedure. The experience from Travelhack 2014 is to market the alternative to vote towards the targeted voters and use this communication need as one part of the marketing campaign to promote the contest to stakeholders and society. One lesson learned is that the crowd-sourcing evaluation method is appropriate when the contest theme addresses challenges that the intended users experience in their everyday life.

Compared to the goals presented in Chap. 5, crowd-sourcing evaluation is suitable when the aim is to increase awareness of societal and commercial challenges where open data and digital services can be used. It is also suitable when the purpose is to strengthen the brand image of the organiser.

11.6 The Mixed Method Evaluation Approach

The mixed method approach combines two or more of the previous five methods into a composite evaluation method. The combination can be sequential or parallel, see Fig. 11.1. If sequential, then one basic evaluation method is used to assess the contributions from one phase and then another assessment is performed at a later phase with another evaluation method. This can be useful, for example, if an ideas phase attracts a large number of submissions that must be reduced due to restrictions in the following service design phase. Organiser driven assessment can thus be used to assess the contributions from the first phase and then the prototypes developed during the second phase can be evaluated using another evaluation method. Travelhack 2013 used this approach. Twenty-four teams with ideas were singled out from a pool of nearly sixty contributions in a first idea phase. These twenty-four teams were invited to the service design phase, which was ended with a

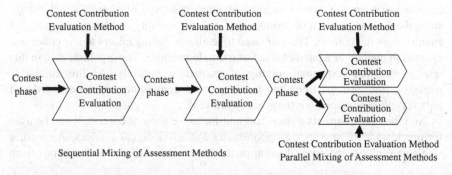

Fig. 11.1 Sequential and parallel mixing of evaluation methods

24-h hackathon that aimed to boost the prototype development. An expert jury then assessed the teams participating at the hackathon to select the final winners.

In the parallel combination, two or more evaluation methods are used in parallel to single out winners at the same time. For example, an expert jury evaluation and a peer review evaluation can be used at the same time, either to single out winners in two contest categories or to single out one winner in the contest by accumulating the scores from the parallel evaluations. During the ElectriCity Innovation Challenge 2015, parallel evaluation was used to determine both the main winner award and the developers' award in the contest. Peer review scoring was, in this case, used to define the developers' award and the main winner award was determined through the use of an expert-jury.

Compared to the contest goals presented in Chap. 5, mixed method evaluation is suitable when the goal is to develop alliances with complementary partners where deep interaction is necessary for successful innovation. In this case, the contest can provide the means for strengthening an innovation community to which the organiser belongs. It can also stimulate the use of a platform that supports forming alliances and interaction between developers. In order to select potential alliance partners, a single evaluation may not be enough.

11.7 Methods for Evaluating Contest Contributions Vis-à-Vis Contest Formats

Four types of open digital innovation contests were introduced in Chap. 3. An innovation jam is a short contest and very inclusive in terms of participation; it is especially useful for generating many new ideas. In this type of contest, one single evaluation method might be preferable, as the short time frame for the contest limits the possibility of arranging multiple evaluations. If the organiser of an innovation jam would like to use multiple evaluation methods, then the parallel model of mixed evaluation methods is preferable as this enables concurrent evaluation that can be time-boxed within the scarce time available in a jam.

An innovation cup is similar to an innovation jam in being inclusive, but it is extended in time, e.g. weeks or even months. This type of contest is helpful for strengthening an innovation community and the solidity in the prototypes that emerge from the contest. The increased time allows the organisers to use either one evaluation method or a parallel setup of multiple methods. The organiser can, in this setting, also use sequential mixing of evaluation methods. As this format is inclusive and aims to strengthen the innovation community, crowd sourced and peer review evaluations are particularly relevant.

An innovation battle is a short and non-inclusive form of contest. It can be used for quickly identifying strong opportunities for novel digital services. As such, a single carefully prepared evaluation method is preferred. If the contributions from the contest permit, then the automated evaluation method may be preferable in this situation. Other relevant methods are the organiser based evaluation method and the expert jury.

An innovation challenge is an extended and non-inclusive contest; it can help an organiser to decide whether to build or procure. Consequently, the contest may be used as part of a procurement process or as an initiator to a development process, with the objective of creating a new digital service to be launched on an end-user market. This setup calls for a sequential evaluation method that involves multiple evaluations and perhaps a mixing of methods. If the contest is a part of a procurement process, then a pre-screening of ideas may be appropriate using the organiser-based evaluation method, followed by an expert jury or an organiser based evaluation of the final results.

11.8   "And the Winner Is…": Communicating the Evaluation Outcome

After having evaluated the contest contributions, an important task is to communicate the evaluation results. An open digital innovation process that has been organised as a contest can accumulate enormous amounts of expectations from participants, beneficiaries and other stakeholders.

Who won? What won? Why did we not win? What are the strengths in the solutions and what are the weaknesses? These are examples of questions that need to be answered. At the end of the final, all light will be on the winner or the winners of the contest, the awarding of the prizes and the justifications of the evaluations. However, communicating the evaluation outcome is not only about announcing and celebrating the winner, but it also includes communicating the results, the contribution and providing feedback to the other participants.

The use of an automated evaluation method will enable the contest organisers to link the evaluation to a digital result board that communicates the results during the competition as well as the final outcome of the contest. The Contest Support Platform, see Chap. 8, could be a vehicle for such a board. The platform can also be used to present the winners of the contest and communicate what type of prototype won, justifications for why the prototype won, the prize and what happens now. Such communication is valuable as it creates confidence in the contest regardless of the evaluation method adopted. For the winners, this type of public information is also an important part of the prize, i.e. to be openly acknowledged as a winner by the contest organisers.

Experiences from Travelhack 2011, Travelhack 2013 and the Volvo Car Challenge 2013 indicate that individual feedback to each participating team is important to stimulate continuation of development and as a response to the expectations of the participants. This individual feedback is preferably an accumulation of the strengths, weaknesses, challenges and opportunities that the evaluation has generated.

11.9 Activity Description

Evaluate Contest Contributions is the third activity in the contest phase. The purpose of the evaluation activity is to identify the most valuable and promising contributions that have been submitted by the participants. Four sub-activities constitute the activity, which are linked to other activities in the pre-contest phase, more specifically, *Set goals*, *Engage Stakeholders*, *Design contest* and *Develop platform*.

11.9.1 Sub-activities

1. Select evaluation methods:

   a. review contest goals and contest design and select appropriate assessment approach: single or multiple assessments;
   b. review contest goals and select appropriate evaluation methods.

2. Prepare assessment activities:

   a. adapt the selected evaluation methods:

      i. review contest goals as well as contest design and define evaluation criteria;
      ii. define how teams should submit and present their contributions for evaluation;
      iii. develop instruments for evaluating contributions:

          1. prepare how to evaluate contributions and develop or adopt an evaluation tool (organiser driven, expert jury);
          2. develop and implement an evaluation algorithm (automated);
          3. develop a guide for supporting peers or the crowd in evaluating contributions and implement a tool for collecting and storing peer evaluations (peer review, crowd source);

      iv. organise the decision process; how to reach a result and, if applicable, merge results.

   b. Organise the specific assessment activities:

      i. organiser-driven and expert-jury evaluation:

         1. staff evaluation group;
         2. anchor evaluation criteria, scoring and evaluation tool;
         3. ensure participation in assessment activity;
         4. determine the division of labour;
         5. sync. assessment with how and when teams should submit contributions for assessment.

  ii. Peer-review evaluation method:

    1. inform the participants about the peer review process and the guidelines;
    2. allocate time for the peer review after the contest is closed.

 iii. Crowd-sourcing evaluation method:

    1. market the chance to participate in the evaluation;
    2. mobilise the crowd to participate in the evaluation.

 c. Define how to communicate the outcome from assessment activities:

  1. review contest goals and define what, when and how results/feedback should be provided to participants;
  2. prepare if and how results/feedback are provided to the participants during the contest (e.g. positions);
  3. prepare how results/feedback are provided to participants during the contest finale (e.g. winner announcement);
  4. prepare how results/feedback are provided to participants (e.g. final results) via the contest support platform and other channels, if applicable;
  5. prepare how results/feedback are provided to participants individually after the contest (e.g. strengths, weaknesses, challenges, opportunities).

3. Conduct assessment activities:

 a. inform participating teams about the deadline and ensure submission of contributions;
 b. make contributions available:

   i. make contributions available to the jury (organiser driven, expert jury);
   ii. make contributions available to evaluation algorithm (automated);
  iii. make contributions available to peers or crowd (peer review, crowd).

 c. Perform evaluations including the mobilisation of peers or crowd for peer review and crowd source;
 d. review evaluation results and make a decision about the contest outcome.

4. Communicate assessment activities:

 a. if applicable, provide results/feedback to participants during the contest (e.g. positions, live result boards);
 b. provide results/feedback to participants during the mid-term or contest finale (e.g. winner announcement, results);
 c. provide results/feedback (e.g. final results) via the contest support platform and other channels, if applicable;
 d. provide results/feedback to participants individually after the contest (e.g. strengths, weaknesses, challenges, opportunities).

11.10   Running Examples

In Travelhack 2011, an Innovation Jam, contributions were evaluated with the support of two methods in a parallel assessment setting. The contest was a 24-h event that ended with a final presentation in which the twenty participating teams presented their contributions to an expert jury, fellow developers and an invited audience of stakeholders. The aim of the contest was to challenge external developers to develop digital service prototypes, based on open data that would stimulate travellers to travel more sustainably using e.g. public transport or bicycle. The evaluation methods used were the expert jury and the peer review model. In order to prepare these two evaluations, a set of criteria were developed prior to the contest with a score-board, which enabled the jury to score the contributions. The criteria and the score-board were presented to the expert jury two weeks before the contest in order to anchor the model and jointly revise the assessment tool. This prepared the jury in terms of using the evaluation instrument.

The contest was a weekend live event that started at noon on Saturday and ended at noon on Sunday. Presentations began after the deadline was reached and the participants had uploaded their contributions on Trafiklab.se, which constituted the contest support platform. The presentations proceeded for one and a half hours and were then followed by a jury discussion where scores were compared and contributions reviewed. A lesson learned is that a balance must be reached between the extent of the scoreboard, the tools used to summarise the scores and the time available for the jury to discuss and decide. Experiences from jury members participating at Travelhack 2011 indicate that they wanted to have more time to discuss the pros and cons of different solutions and thus use their expert knowledge to assess jointly the contributions. However, the focus during this contest, became, instead, scoring and comparing scores, rather than expert knowledge driven assessment.

In parallel to the expert driven assessment, the participants themselves assessed their fellow participants' contributions. This was organised via the contest support platform, through which the participants could review the contributions submitted. One team had one vote and was not allowed to vote for their own team. The results from both evaluations were then announced to the participants and the prizes were handed out to the winners. After the contest, only brief feedback was provided to the participating teams including the final results. A lesson learned from this was that the teams that do not win are not that interested in their ranking. This information has some value but, more interesting for a team is to receive feedback about the strengths and weaknesses of their contribution.

The lessons learned from organising Travelhack 2011 were used in the organisation of Travelhack 2013, an Innovation Cup and the Volvo Truck Open Innovation Challenge 2015. In these contests, expert jury driven evaluation was used as the evaluation method. In Travelhack 2013, time was allocated for the expert jury to develop both an in-depth understanding about the teams and their contributions prior to the presentation after the contest deadline and the structured jury review. The jury duty started when the hackathon started and included the possibility for jury members to talk with the teams during the contest and in situ. Develop an understanding about team and solution progress. Although rigid, the evaluation criteria and the score-board used were more applicable compared to the one at Travelhack 2011, with the consequence that the jury could be focused on discussing the contributions, not merely summarising the scores.

This enhanced approach was improved further during the Volvo Truck Open Innovation Challenge 2015 by introducing a digital tool to organise the final discussion to compare the comments and the scores given by different jury members. The use of the digital tool structured the expert knowledge driven discussion further and made the decision process more efficient. Another lesson learned from this contest was the need, during evaluation, of a capacity to adapt how the evaluation is organised in order to keep to the time schedule and ensure a fair process where every participating team has the same conditions in which to present their contributions to the jury members. The original time schedule for individual presentations of the solutions after the deadline did not include time for teams to set up their preparations. This problem was resolved by moving the jury between two rooms. When one team was making their presentation to the jury, the next team was setting up their presentation in a parallel room. The expert jury consequently shifted between these two rooms and the time schedule was saved, even allocating more time for the concluding jury discussion.

Chapter 12
Develop Strategy

Abstract In this chapter, we present the activity *Develop strategy*. The goal of the activity is to develop a strategy that guides the organisers in managing participant relationships after the end of a contest. First, we discuss strategic options for the post contest phase. The strategic options range from not establishing relationships at all to providing substantial support for selected participants enabling close and long-term relationships. Then we present the activity with running examples for different strategic options. Finally, we give some suggestions for further reading.

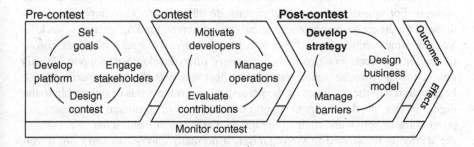

When the contest ends, the organisers can choose how to continue the relationships with the former participants. By doing so, organisers can support the participants in overcoming some of the barriers they face in service deployment, see Chap. 13. The first strategic choice is related to whether the resources made available to the participants for the contest should remain available to them after the contest. For example, if the APIs and open data remain available, the former participants can implement and deliver services based on these. However, if these resources are withdrawn when the contest ends, it may not be possible for them to transform their prototypes to operational services. In Fig. 12.1, these two strategic options are labelled A and B.

The second choice is about additional support to the former participants, or more often to a select number of them, normally the winners of the contest. The extent of

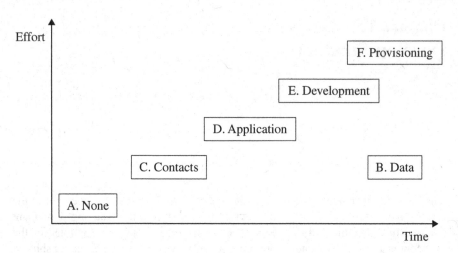

Fig. 12.1 Strategic options for the post contest process

post contest support varies a lot between organisers. For option C, organisers offer information and contacts. A few examples are to offer former participants to partake in events organised for possible sponsors, or to be presented to contacts who can help in further developing the solution, or to nominate former participants to other contests. For option D, former participants are offered support to apply for development funding and competence, often from different funding agencies, such as Sweden's innovation agency,[1] but also from other sources such as larger corporations or sponsors. For option E, organisers offer development support. In this option, the rights to the digital service can either stay with the former participant or be transferred to the organiser. If the participant keeps the rights of ownership to the digital service, the development support often consists of enrolment in a mentorship programme or help with refining the product. On the other hand, if the ownership of the service is transferred to the organiser, it normally chooses to carry out development without involving the former participant. For option F, the organiser of the contest takes full responsibility to implement the service and make it available to the market.

12.1 Strategies Related to Open Innovation

The strategic options presented in Fig. 12.1 represent different ways to engage in open innovation. The first four options (A, B, C and D) are related to inside-out types of open innovation, see Fig. 12.2. The organisers support former participants

---

[1]www.vinnova.se.

Fig. 12.2 The relationship between strategic options and innovation types. The corresponding open innovation capacity in italic

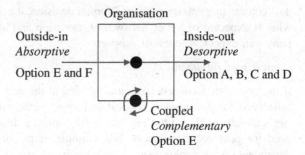

with resources from within their own organisations. These resources are provided by the organisers to support external developers in transferring their prototypes to viable digital services.

Option E is partly related to coupled innovation where the external developers and the organisers contribute with complementary knowledge, using their connective capacity, to deploy the open digital service. In the case where ownership is transferred from external developers to organisers, the type of innovation is rather outside-in than coupled. In this case the service prototype is used as input to the organiser's innovation processes. The same goes for option F where the service prototype is deployed and provided on a service market by the organiser, using its absorptive capacity.

12.2   Activity Description

In this activity, organisers of open digital innovation contests develop a strategy for post-contest support that they will provide and they organise the resources necessary for providing this support.

12.2.1   Sub-activities

- Prepare strategy decision;
- formulate and communicate strategy for post contest support;
- organise resources to match the chosen level of support.

12.2.1.1   Prepare Strategy Decision

Before an organiser formulates the strategy, he or she needs to collect and compile information from several areas to make an informed decision about the scope of post contest support. By making a formal decision, it becomes clear to the organiser what is expected of his or her own organisation and also what the former participants can expect in terms of support.

Contest goal fulfilment

If the organiser's contest goals are fulfilled at the end of the contest, then there is little need for post contest support to former participants. However, if the organiser's contest goals are not met when the contest is finished, then there might be a need for post contest support. For example, if the organiser's goal fulfilment is dependent on the deployment of the participants' services, then the organiser could benefit from supporting them in the transformation process.

Evaluation of the prototypes

The evaluation of the prototypes provides important information about the quality and market potential of the open digital services. However, a specific organiser might find some services more interesting and more aligned with their own goals than the service prototype that formally won the contest.

Status and business goals of the former participants

External developers participate in open digital innovation contests for various reasons and in different arrangements. In order to make an informed decision about the prospect of working together with former participants, it is important for an organiser to understand their corporate form, business performance and business goals. Only then is it possible for the organiser to evaluate if they would make a good fit with his or her own goals and organisation.

Potential benefits of the deployed services

The contest and the evaluation of the submitted service prototypes may have involved market plans and business models. However, when moving from contest to service deployment, it is important to re-evaluate these plans and relate them to the organiser's own goals.

Organiser's open innovation capacity

As mentioned in Chap. 5, the open innovation capacity of the organiser consists of absorptive capacity related to the ability to organise for and make use of the knowledge gained through an outside-in type of open innovation, a complementary capacity related to the ability to participate in and gain knowledge created in coupled innovation and the capacity related to the ability to organise for the use of internal knowledge and resources by external partners. As different options for support to former participants require different open innovation capacities, as illustrated in Fig. 12.2, it is important that the organiser scrutinises his or her own abilities in this regard.

12.2.1.2 Formulate and Communicate Strategy for Post Contest Support

Based on the information compiled in the previous sub-activity, the organiser formulates his or her strategy for post-contest support. The different strategic options, as illustrated in Fig. 12.1, serve as input to this decision. A budget is allocated to implement the strategy. The size of the budget depends primarily on the potential benefits of the selected open digital services. The strategy is communicated externally to the former participants, as well as internally to the groups and individuals affected by the decision.

12.2.1.3 Organise Resources to Match the Decided Level of Support

The strategy decided in the previous sub-activity will require human, technical and monetary resources in order to be realised. Depending on the scope of the strategy, different parts of the organisation will become involved in its execution. For example, if an organiser decides to keep the open data resources available to a select number of former participants (option B), then resources need to be allocated for maintenance of the open data repository. Supporting former participants with information and contacts (option C) will require people appointed to provide these resources. Experience from several open digital innovation contests show that already this low level of post-contest support can be very useful to external developers.

12.3 Guideline

- Make an active choice regarding strategy for post-contest support to former participants.

Organisers create a lot of interest and buzz through open digital innovation contests. In order for promising service prototypes to be transformed into viable services in an open data market, organisers need to make clear their position after the contest. By doing so, participants as well as members of the organisations know what to expect and what types of relationships they should establish.

12.4 Running Examples

In Table 12.1 examples of digital innovation contests are presented for each of the strategic options.

Table 12.1 Examples of digital innovation contests for each of the strategic options

Option	Description	Example
A	Resources from contest not made available	Volvo Car Challenge
B	Resources from contest remain available	Apps4Ottawa 2013
C	Information and contacts	Apps for Europe 2014
D	Support to apply for development competence and funding	Travelhack13
E1	Development support, kept ownership	Open Data Challenge Series 2015
E2	Development support, transferred ownership	Take Action Open Data Challenge 2013
F	Service provisioning	Apps4Finland

12.5   Read More

Organisers of open digital innovation contests take on the role as innovation intermediaries (Juell-Skielse et al. 2014). Depending on which strategic option organisers choose, they perform different functions of an innovation intermediary, see Table 12.2. The functions are based on the framework presented by Howells (2006).

For options A and B organisers do not provide any functions as innovation intermediaries.

The strategic option C relates to an innovation intermediary's function to filter out promising participants and ideas or prototypes to other contests or to support participants with contacts, *Scanning and information processing*. It also relates to

Table 12.2 The innovation intermediary functions of the different strategic options for post-contest support

Option	Description	Intermediary functions
A	Resources from contest not available	None
B	Resources from contest remain	None
C	Information and contacts	• Scanning and information processing • Knowledge processing, generation and combination
D	Support to apply for development competence and funding	• Gatekeeping and brokering • Commercialisation: exploiting the outcomes
E	Development support	• Testing, validation and training • Intellectual property: protecting the results
F	Service provisioning	• Commercialisation: exploiting the outcomes

the function of sharing information and combining knowledge of several partners, *Knowledge processing, generation and combination*.

The strategic option D relates to the support discussed for level C but the organiser takes greater responsibility for establishing the relationships, moving towards brokering of contracts, *Gatekeeping and brokering*. Moreover, the support is of a more commercial nature resembling the functions of finding potential capital funding and organising applications to retrieve funds, *Commercialisation: exploiting the outcomes*.

For option E the organisers share a greater amount of the development risks and perform the intermediary functions associated with the previous levels but also *Testing, validation and training* and with *Intellectual property: protecting the results*.

In option F the organisers offer comprehensive support related to marketing and sales and public offerings associated with *Commercialisation: exploiting the outcomes* as well as the intermediary functions of the lower levels.

To summarise, during post-contest support, organisers perform additional functions as well as functions at a greater scale associated with innovation intermediaries. These functions primarily pertain to filtering and sharing of contacts as well as supporting funding and commercialisation.

References

Howells, J. (2006). Intermediation and the role of intermediaries in innovation. *Research Policy, 35*(5), 715–728.

Juell-Skielse, G., Hjalmarsson, A., Juell-Skielse, E., Johannesson, P., & Rudmark, D. (2014). Contests as innovation intermediaries in open data markets. *Information Polity, 19*(3, 4), 247–262.

Chapter 13
Manage Innovation Barriers

Abstract This chapter deals with how innovation barriers after a contest can be managed if the organizer of the contest has decided to provide support also after the contest itself has ended. As starting point, a survey of such barriers to innovation is presented together with approaches for managing such barriers. The management approach is described from a contest organizers perspective, and includes an activity description followed by a running example. Finally, a read more section presents the theoretical base for the innovation barrier approach. *Manage Innovation Barriers* is the second activity in the post contest phase. After the contest, the deployment of a digital service will be structured according to a decided post contest strategy. See Chap. 12, *Develop strategy*, for managing the relationship between the organisers and the former participants. Different barriers can hinder a post contest deployment project to transform a prototype to an operational digital service ready for market entry.

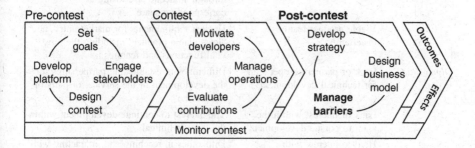

An often-perceived problem is that organisations, as well as societies, are insufficiently innovative, including difficulties associated with generating innovative ideas and prototypes. Other problems pertain to the transformation of initial innovations into products, and the resistance to adopting innovations that are ready for deployment. One approach to viewing such problems is to see them as innovation barriers, i.e., constraints or factors that inhibit innovation. Similarly, one could view

© Springer International Publishing AG 2017
A. Hjalmarsson et al., *Open Digital Innovation*, Progress in IS,
DOI 10.1007/978-3-319-56339-8_13

Table 13.1 Innovation barriers in post contest service deployment

Barrier		Meaning
Finance	Lack of time or money to prepare market entry	Time and money are scarce resources and an obvious challenge for teams transforming early innovations into products
	Lack of external funding to reach market entry	The team has difficulty in attracting external financing, such as venture capital or government innovation funds
	Lack of model to generate revenues to sustain the service	The team has difficulty in developing a revenue model that enables the team to sustain the service after market entry
Knowledge	Lack of marketing competence and market information	The team does not possess enough market knowledge for the developed service, nor the skills to develop market understanding
	Lack of technical competence and innovation experience	No previous experience of innovation and a shortage of necessary technical expertise in the team
	Difficulties finding competent team members	A shortage of candidates to fill competence gaps within the team
Market	Weak value offering	The customer benefits offered by the service developed by the team are unclear or poorly articulated
	Multifaceted market conditions and uncertain product demand	The market for the solution is unclear and the demand for the service is uncertain
	High market competition and saturation	A high level of competition in a market where the only way to gain market share is through someone else losing a corresponding share
	Viable product features uncertainty	Unclear requirements for market entry, i.e., "least viable product" including the most vital functions and features
Organisation	Lack of partner co-operation for technical development	Difficulties in establishing partnerships for the development of the service, or parts of the service
	Lack of interest within the team to pursue development	The interest to continue development within the team is limited
	Hard to interact with infrastructure and data providers	Difficulties in reaching and interacting with the organisations that provide open resources such as data, infrastructure and platforms
	Difficulties establishing licences for APIs and other services	Challenges in establishing the agreements with suppliers for the use of the necessary data, protocols and services
	Lack of partner co-operation for technical tests	Difficulties in including external partners such as data or service providers for the team to test their own service thoroughly
	Lack of partner co-operation for knowledge transfer	Insufficient co-operation with partners who can support knowledge transfer

(continued)

Table 13.1 (continued)

Barrier		Meaning
Regulation	Inefficient intellectual property processes	The team has difficulties in protecting the rights to their service innovation
	Hindering industry structures	The viability of the service is contingent on finding creative ways of dealing with e.g., licensing, regulations or industry agreements
Technology	Varieties of platforms requiring unique service development	The service has to be developed and maintained in several versions for different types of devices, including smartphones, tablets and cars
	Difficulties in reaching adequate technical quality in the service	Challenges related to technical development and the ability to design a service of high technical quality
	Lack of quality in used open digital resources	The service requires external resources that are available, but are lacking in quality which negatively affects the service
	Needed digital resources are missing	The service requires certain external resources that are not available to the service provider
	Changes in used APIs at short notice	The service is dependent on external resources that are provided, but the provider makes changes at short notice which hamper service deployment
	Limitations in existing service-dependent platforms	Deficiencies and lack of functionality in, e.g., operating systems for mobile phones or web-browsers that the team depends on

innovation enablers as success factors that facilitate innovation. Thus, barriers and success factors can often be seen as two sides of the same coin, e.g., when the presence of a resource counts as a success factor, while its absence is seen as a barrier. By viewing problems as barriers, organisations can recognise constraints that hinder their innovation processes. They can then design solutions to cope with the barriers and thereby make the innovation process more efficient and value creating.

Hjalmarsson et al. (2014, 2015) investigated what kind of innovation barriers affect the post contest phase when a development team transforms a prototype to a market-ready digital service. The longitudinal investigation resulted in a list of twenty-four innovation barriers, grouped into six categories, c.f. Table 13.1.

The study shows that developers face innovation barriers in three stages after an innovation contest: activation, building development momentum and preparing market entry.

In the *activation* stage, which starts directly after the contest, the survey shows that developers mainly struggle to mobilise free time or financial resources in order to continue the development of their prototype. In this stage, developers also work to understand the market demands of their solution and they start to craft a value offering that is attractive for the targeted market.

Those developers, who are able to pass the activation stage, enter into a second stage, in which *development momentum* needs to be mobilised. The survey indicates that developers who are able to focus on their prototype at least two months after the contest have a good chance of entering this stage (Hjalmarsson et al. 2015). The barriers developers now face are, again, lack of time and resources. Moreover, lack of external funding can hamper developers at this stage, as well as a lack of an operative revenue model to generate future resources. If developers are able to make progress in development, other barriers may also surface during this stage, in particular, the lack of quality in service contingent open data and challenges to ensure adequate quality in the service. Developers also have an increased need now to interact with data providers, to request data and receive support. They also need to understand customers' basic requirements in order to identify the most vital functions and features in their solution.

If barriers can be managed and development momentum is established, the longitudinal survey (Hjalmarsson et al. 2015) indicates that developers will enter the third stage, *preparing market entry*. In this stage, developers focus on assuring the quality of the most important features of their solution. As the momentum within the team is high, financial and motivational barriers can easily be managed. Instead, developers struggle with external technological barriers, e.g., missing data for the service, lack of quality in open data needed or changes in APIs (Application Programming Interfaces) at short notice. Furthermore, developers need to address internal technical barriers, e.g., difficulties in reaching adequate quality in the service being finalised, as well as a lack of partner co-operation for tests and knowledge transfer.

13.1   Barrier Management

Barrier management comprises different measures that organisers of open digital innovation contests can take in order to support the post-contest phase. The key measures are:

1. scout barriers;
2. mark up barriers;
3. pilot barriers;
4. dredge barriers.

Scout barriers means that the organiser systematically charts the post-contest phase with the aim of identifying barriers. This identification of barriers can be done prior to service deployment and de-coupled from the teams in the contest. It can also be provided as a service from the organiser to the teams during the post-contest phase, i.e., the organiser provides support in situ to the deployment teams. The approach adopted for barrier scouting is dependent on the involvement of the organiser in the post-contest deployment project, as discussed in Chap. 12.

Mark up barriers is the second measure to provide assistance to service deployment projects. The marking up of barriers identifies the approximate positions of different barriers in the development process, as well as their characteristics and possible effects. The measure provides the deployment project with a post-contest chart where barriers are marked, thereby informing developers about challenges that need to be addressed.

The contest organiser can, in addition to barrier scouting and barrier mark up, also choose to actively engage itself in navigating the post contest project to pass one or several barriers. This measure, *pilot barriers*, requires that the organiser makes a strategic choice to provide active support to the developers after the contest. In terms of the strategic options of Chap. 12, pilot barriers mean that at least *D. Application* support is provided by the organiser. Application support means that former participants are offered support to apply for development funding and competence. It could, for example, be that the organiser supports the deployment project to attract external funding, thereby passing the barrier that team members lack time or money to proceed with development.

Dredge barriers is the fourth barrier management measure. When applied by the organiser, recurrent constraints are removed to facilitate service deployment. The effort to dredge barriers could either be a consequence of barrier scouting or follow the provision of the pilot service to the development team. During these activities, barriers might be observed that should be removed rather than navigated around. One example is the lack of quality in provided open data, which could be removed permanently rather than recurrently navigated, in order to enhance the value in the solution provided. The removal of barriers might require that other stakeholders besides the development team and the organiser become involved, for example, resource providers if the barrier is related to provision of open digital resources.

13.2   Activity Description

The activity, *Manage Innovation Barriers*, aims to support organisers to decide how to support the deployment project. The provision of support to manage barriers is dependent on the relationship between the organiser and the deployment team and, thus, the level of support decided. This means that the organisers' involvement in coping with innovation barriers may range from no involvement at all to strong involvement to scout out, manage or actively remove barriers.

13.2.1   Sub-activities

- Analyse the impact of the strategy adopted for the relationship between the organisers and the former participants, see Chap. 12.

- Determine organiser degree of involvement in the management of barriers.

- *No involvement* (option A. None and B. Data); the organisers provide no support in barrier management, i.e., it is up to the deployment project to cope with any barrier that may surface.
- *Passive involvement* (option C. Contacts); the organisers provide passive support in barrier management, e.g., by providing information about barriers that are likely to appear, or by providing advice on how to cope with barriers related to funding or use of open data.
- *Active involvement* (option D. Application E. Development and F. Provisioning); the organisers provide active support to scout, mark up, pilot and dredge barriers when they appear.

• Select mode for organiser involvement in barrier management:

- *proactive approach*; the organisers are ahead of the post contest process to scout and mark up barriers. If applicable, identified barriers may also be removed before service deployment starts.
- *reactive barrier management*; the organisers in this mode are on stand-by and provide barrier management support to the deployment project when barriers surface.

• Plan when the organiser should participate in barrier management:

- *before the post contest process*; barrier management is, in this case, performed ahead of the post contest process. Organisers support future projects by scouting out and marking up barriers and, if possible and relevant, by removing barriers;
- *throughout the post contest process*; in this case, support is provided during the post contest process from start to end. This case is a likely model if the organiser is heavily involved in the deployment project. It involves, for example, proactive piloting to avoid barriers as well as reactive coping of constraints when they emerge.
- Periodically support during the post contest process:

  in the activation stage; support provided to cope with barriers hindering the development project from restarting development after the contest;
  in building up development momentum; support provided to cope with barriers affecting the project so as to transform efficiently the contest contribution into a viable solution;
  in preparing for market entry; support provided to cope with barriers to complete the solution and prepare for market entry.

- *After the post contest process*; in this case, the organisers review lessons learned from the specific development process in order to mark up barriers ahd, if applicable, remove barriers that are likely to affect future projects.

• Adopt and use appropriate barrier management measures to characterise and cope with constraints:

- scout barriers that may affect the development project;
- define and characterise surfaced and potential barriers;

what characterises the barrier, what causes it to happen and what is the effect?
How can and should the barrier be managed?
Who has the lead responsibility for managing the barrier?

13.3 Running Example

Travelhack 2013 was a contest with a twofold purpose: (1) to increase the use of the open data platform Trafiklab.se and (2) to stimulate developers to pursue the development of novel digital services to make public transport more attractive in the Stockholm region. This objective was divided into four intended effects:

- five novel digital services, easy to use, that enable smart public transport use.
- One hundred and fifty participants (20–30 teams) at the final event.
- Two services that were actively in development and in use one year after the contest.
- One service that has reached the top ten in the most downloaded services in the travel category in Sweden three years after the contest (AppStore/Android Market).

During the final 24 h hackathon, twenty-one teams finalised their service ideas into prototypes, and an expert-jury selected the winners. The team behind the digital service, Resledaren, won both the category for making public transport more accessible to everyone and the overall winner's prize. The organisers had no intention of acquiring any of the contributions. However, by the defined set of criteria for evaluation and using an expert jury to select winners, they deliberately ruled the outcome with the aim of pointing out the services with the highest potential to become viable. Furthermore, the organisers offered active support to the winner jointly to apply for funding of a collaborative service innovation project (funded by the Swedish government agency for innovation, vinnova). The organisers' primary motive for the latter was to:

> …promote the development, launch and marketing of the winning submission as a viable open data service (Resledaren) that enables people with cognitive dysfunctions to access and use public transportation, and investigate how such collaboration is organized with the aim to develop sustainable capability to recurrent organize cost-effective open digital innovation on large scale.

In the Autumn of 2013, the consortium with the winning team and the organisers, as key stakeholders, received funding for the joint project (€150,000). And in September, 2014 the first version of Resledaren was launched on Google Play and the iOS App. Store. During the period from Autumn 2013 to Autumn 2014, the organisers decided to become actively involved in the transformation of Resledaren as a proto-type to Resledaren as a launch solution. The involvement meant that they provided support throughout the process according to the strategy, option D. application, described in Chap. 12. The main responsibility for managing barriers in the post contest phase was the development team. However, the organisers provided support, both proactively and reactively, to scout and navigate barriers that emerged throughout the post contest phase. For example, a number of technology barriers related to the open data were scouted, which resulted in strategies to work around them and also improvements in the provided data. Another example of barrier management was the involvement of the organisers in securing initial funding for the project.

13.4   Read More

There exists a vast amount of literature on innovation barriers as well as the related notion of success factors for innovation (Becker and Dietz 2004; Lee et al. 2010). Barriers have been studied at different levels of innovation, from the individual to the firm, sector and country level (King 1990). From a static point of view, barriers are antecedents to innovation, but Hadjimanolis (2003) argues that the nature of barriers is dynamic, evolutionary and complementary and that their effects on innovation are combined. For example, certain barriers act at different stages of the innovation process and some barriers intermediate the effects of other barriers. The impact of a barrier is determined by the stage of innovation at which it acts as well as the mechanism of action (Hadjimanolis 2003). Hjalmarsson et al. (2014, 2015) adapted the barriers approach to innovation to the context of open digital innovation contests.

References

Becker, W., & Dietz, J. (2004). R&D cooperation and innovation activities of firms—evidence for the German manufacturing industry. *Research Policy, 33*(2), 209–223.

Hadjimanolis, A. (2003). *The barriers approach to innovation. The international handbook on innovation.* Oxford: Elsevier Science.

Hjalmarsson, A., Johannesson, P., Juell-Skielse, G., & Rudmark, D. (2014). Beyond innovation contests: A framework of barriers to open innovation of digital services.

Hjalmarsson, A., Juell-Skielse, G., Ayele, W. Y., Rudmark, D., & Johannesson, P. (2015, May). From contest to market entry: A longitudinal survey of innovation barriers constraining open data service development. *In ECIS 2015.*

King, N. (1990). Innovation at work: The research literature. In M. West & J. Farr (Eds.), *Innovation and creativity at work* (pp. 15–59). Chichester: Wiley.

Lee, S., Park, G., Yoon, B., & Park, J. (2010). Open innovation in SMEs—An intermediated network model. *Research Policy, 39*(2), 290–300.

Chapter 14
Design Business Model

Abstract In this chapter, we discuss how organisers design or adapt business models to clarify how contest goals and service deployment contribute to their business. First, we present how the formulated strategy, see Chap. 12, affects the business model. Then we describe and give some guidelines for the activity *Design business model*. Finally, we present examples of each of the proposed business model types.

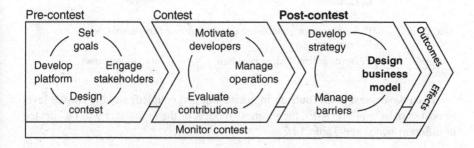

Business models are used to explain the business logic of organisations, i.e. how they create and capture value in relation to other organisations. A business model could be thought of as a common language for expressing the characteristics of a firm's business logic, but also as an instrument to change the business logic as a response to market opportunities. Conceptually, a business model consists of a few core components: value proposition, value architecture, value network and value finance, see Table 14.1.

Table 14.1 Business model core components (Ranerup et al. 2016, p. 7)

Component	Characteristics
Value Proposition (VP)	Factors related to the offer of services, products, and activities that create value for users
Value Architecture (VA)	Factors related to how resources (tangible or intangible) are constructed in order to create value for users (e.g., technological configurations and organizational structure)
Value Network (VN)	Factors related to actors (internal and external) and their roles in the transactions in actor-to-actor collaboration
Value Finance (VF)	Factors related to finance, ownership, and costs

Table 14.2 Impact on business model for different types of contest goals and level of post contest support

Contest goal	Strategic option	Impact on business model
Inside-out	A. None	No impact
	B. Data	Open data resource provider
	C. Contacts D. Application	Catalyst
Outside-in	E. Development, (transferred ownership) F. Provisioning	Service provider
Coupled	E. Development, (kept ownership)	Innovation partner

Given the contest goals (outside-in, inside-out and coupled) and the chosen level of post-contest support (A–F), the business models of the organisers will be affected in different ways, see Table 14.2.

14.1   Open Data Resource Provider

Open data resource providers offer open data sets to developers. Developers enrich this data by producing linked data and end user services or applications. In order to become an open data resource provider trusted by developers, an organiser must develop value propositions that support accessibility and ease of use as well as clear data maintenance procedures. Moreover, open data resource providers must be responsive to changes in open data needs among developers. Developers' platforms, as discussed in Chap. 8, provide means for organizers to formalise access to and maintenance of procedures for open data.

Table 14.3 Impact on business model for open data resource provider

Open data resource provider—Impact on business model	
Value proposition	Organisers offer open data to external developers. Open data might be a new product for organisers to offer, and external developers might be a new group of customers to organisers
Value architecture	Connects open data from internal and external sources to external developers
Value network	Organisers need to develop procedures for operating and maintaining open data sets. To support external developers effectively, technical platforms may be developed and provided
Value finance	Organisers will face costs for operating and maintaining open data and developers' platforms. Different revenue streams from open data are possible to cover these costs. Access rights to the provided data need to be clarified

14.2 Catalyst

Organisers act as catalysts when they provide former participants with information, knowledge and contacts to be used for further development. Information can be provided by individuals who have contacts with, for example, venture capitalists who are interested in investing in new digital services. Knowledge can be provided as, for example, support in applying for public funding. Knowledge could also be provided as advice to help external developers manage barriers, see Chap. 13. Forms of knowledge exchange can vary depending on the situation, for example, it could be individual meetings and documents. As catalysts, organisers take on the role of innovation intermediaries.

Table 14.4 Impact on business model for catalyst

Catalyst—Impact on business model	
Value proposition	Organisers offer contacts and knowledge to external developers
Value architecture	Connects knowledge and information from an organiser to external developers
Value network	Organisers need to identify and make available knowledge, individuals and information, to external developers. A technical knowledge management platform may be established to support this. Moreover, a point of contact between external developers and internal resources increases the accessibility of the available knowledge
Value finance	Organisers will face costs for making individuals available and for preparing information and arranging meetings. Revenues take different forms; some catalysts receive public funding while others receive equity in external developers' companies in return

14.3 Service Provider

As service providers, organisers take the output from open digital innovation contests and deploy it as digital services. These new services may fit their current service offerings or provide something new that requires changes to/or integration with current value architectures.

14.4 Innovation Partner

As innovation partners, the organisers and the winning team become partners with external developers in coupled innovation. For example, external developers provide additional technical skills to the team while organisers provide complementary support, e.g. market knowledge or financial support during service deployment.

Table 14.5 Impact on business model for open data resource provider

Service provider—Impact on business model	
Value proposition	Organisers offer new digital services to their customers. The new services may complement the organisers' prevailing customer offerings or add something fundamentally new that attracts new groups of customers
Value architecture	Collects, stores, transforms and presents open data to provide value to end users
Value network	Impact depends on whether current processes are able to handle the new digital services or if new processes for operating the services need to be establishe
Value finance	Organisers will face costs for operating and maintaining the digital services. Different forms of revenue streams are possible, like premium and freemium. Intellectual property rights need to be managed when transferring the rights to the service from participants to organisers

Table 14.6 Impact on business model for innovation partner

Innovation partner—Impact on business model	
Value proposition	Organisers value propositions may be affected depending on the outcome of the innovation activities
Value architecture	Connects innovation knowledge and skills between the organisers and the external developer
Value network	Organisers participate in joint innovation with external developers where both parties offer complementary skills. This requires that the organisers' innovation processes are adapted to cater for collaboration with external developers
Value finance	Organisers will face costs for innovation work. These costs should be related to the increase in value open innovation as compared to closed innovation

14.5 Activity Description

There are no particular methods available for developing business models for contest organisers. We refer to common methods like the Business Model Canvas (Osterwalder and Pigneur 2010). However, the discussion above, on how the level of post contest support impacts on organisers' business models, can be used as input when developing new or adapting existing business models.

14.5.1 Sub-activities

1. Select strategic option for post-contest support (see Chap. 12).
2. Analyse impact on organisations' business model, see Tables 14.2, 14.3, 14.4, 14.5 and 14.6.
3. Develop or adapt business model.

14.6 Guidelines

- The activities, Formulate strategy and Develop business model, influence each other and organisers need to handle both activities simultaneously. Tables 14.2, 14.3, 14.4, 14.5 and 14.6 clarify the consequences of the levels of post contest support and what is expected of organisers during service deployment.
- Involve external developers to identify their needs for open data when developing or adapting a business model for an open data resource provider. Often the real needs of open data do not become evident until during detailed development and testing under real world conditions.

14.7 Running Examples

14.7.1 Open Data Resource Provider—Example City of Stockholm

The city of Stockholm used the open digital innovation contest Open Stockholm Award partly to increase awareness of its open data resources. The open data strategy, developed by the city, targets internal users as well as external developers.

Today, the city operates one of Sweden's most comprehensive repositories of municipal open data and has developed procedures for both maintenance and access.

14.7.2 Catalyst—Example Viktoria Swedish ICT

Viktoria Swedish ICT is a research institute that co-organises several open digital innovation contests, like the Olympic City Transport Challenge and the Electricity Innovation Challenge. They use research to provide advice to organisers as well as external developers. They are normally financed through public funding, such as the funding schemes provided by the Swedish Innovation Agency, Vinnova.

14.7.3 Service Provider—Example Volvo Car Corporation

The Volvo Car Corporation used the Volvo Car Challenge to probe the capacity amongst external developers to provide new digital services that enhance Volvo's offers to end customers. One part of the prize was consequently a potential commercial contract with the Volvo Car Corporation to complete and deploy the winning service as an integrated part in Volvo's vehicle fleet.

14.7.4 Innovation Partner—Example HiQ

After TravelHack 2013, the winning team, Resledaren, teamed up with HiQ, a leading Scandinavian communication and IT technology firm, to deploy their winning service. They created a consortium with the organisers of TravelHack 2013, wherein HiQ added project management skills and additional development capacity and the organisers provided advice and support on how to finance the process to deploy the service. This partnership strengthened the winning team to move beyond their innovative idea and transform the winning prototype to a first version of their service launched to end users.

References

Osterwalder, A., & Pigneur, Y. (2010). *Business model generation: A handbook for visionaries, game changers, and challengers*. John Wiley & Sons.
Ranerup, A., Henriksen, H. Z., & Hedman, J. (2016). An analysis of business models in Public Service Platforms. *Government Information Quarterly, 33*(1), 6–14.

Chapter 15
Monitor Contest

Abstract In this chapter, we present a method for evaluating open digital innovation contests. The method serves several purposes: it helps to evaluate whether
the organisers have achieved their goals of organising the contest or not, it supports
managers in managing the contest operations and it supports learning within the
organisations. The activity also supports knowledge transfer to other organisations
and supports making contributions to the scientific knowledge base. The method
description is followed by an example and a few guidelines.

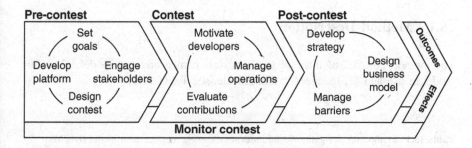

Several models for evaluating innovation have been developed. These models aid
managers to measure and analyse the status and outcomes of innovation. For
example, the Innovation Value Chain by Hansen and Birkinshaw (2007) aids
executives in evaluating innovation processes, identifying specific challenges and
developing ways to manage them. Measurement models for open digital innovation
contests are developed to support organisers in evaluating the status, challenges and
outcomes of a contest.

Since both goals and contest designs vary, the model that is used to monitor and
evaluate a contest has to be designed or adapted for that particular contest. In this
chapter, we present a method for creating such a model. The method uses contest

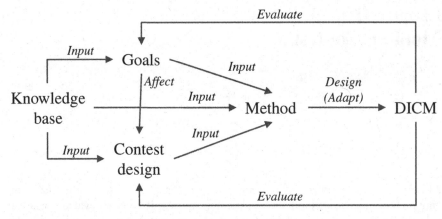

Fig. 15.1 Relationships between goals, contest design, knowledge base and method for measuring digital innovation contests

goals, contest design and lessons learned from previous contests as input for adapting and using a measurement model for a specific contest, see Fig. 15.1, where DICM means Digital Innovation Contest Measurement Model.

15.1   Method Description

The method consists of three phases: (1) design measurement model, (2) refine model in use and (3) learn and communicate, see Table 15.1.

Table 15.1 Method for designing digital innovation contest measurement model (DICM)

Phase	Steps	Output
1. Design measurement model	• Characterise. • Set measurement goals • Build measurement model	Measurement model designed for a specific open digital innovation contest
2. Refine model in use	• Measure • Analyse result • Provide immediate feedback	Evaluated and updated measurement model
3. Learn and communicate	• Analyse • Package • Disseminate	Knowledge: – Specific about particular contest – General, valuable to knowledge base

15.1.1   Phase 1: Design Measurement Model

In this phase, organisers build a measurement model specific to their open digital innovation contest.

15.1.1.1   Step 1. Characterise

In the first step, organisers analyse the characteristics of their innovation contest by reflecting on the contest goals and the specific contest design.

15.1.1.2   Step 2. Set Measurement Goals

In this step, organisers verify the relevance of contest goals and sub-goals, defined in the activity, *Set goals* and evaluate them from the perspective of measurement. If contest goals are vague or difficult to measure, they are redefined and sub-goals are created to facilitate measurement. Moreover, to balance contest goals, organisers can identify relevant perspectives such as finance, innovation and customers. Finally, questions are articulated to clarify when the goals are reached. For example, if a contest goal is to "Increase understanding of open data needs and requirements" then the following question can help in measuring its fulfilment "Which are the five most common open data needs among participants in the contest?"

15.1.1.3   Step 3. Build a Measurement Model

In this step, organisers identify, define and describe processes, phases, inputs, activities, outputs and measures of their measurement model based on characteristics and questions. Measurements are derived from the questions formulated in Step 2. Identification of relevant data sources is also an important activity and the availability of data will constrain the design of the measurement model. The running example presented below may serve as a starting point when organisers design their own model.

15.1.2   Phase 2: Refine Model in Use

In this phase, organisers put the measurement model to use. The use of the model primarily supports the activities *Manage Contest Operations* and *Manage Barriers to Service Deployment*. By using the model, organisers will better understand its strengths and weaknesses and be able to refine its design.

15.1.2.1   Step 1. Measure

In this step, organisers set up processes for capturing data and reporting the measurement results on a timely basis according to the needs of contest management. Measurement results will help contest managers to identify triggers as described in Chap. 10 as well as barriers as described in Chap. 13.

15.1.2.2   Step 2. Analyse Results

In the second step, organisers analyse the results of using the measurement model. Its strengths and weaknesses are identified.

15.1.2.3   Step 3. Provide Immediate Feedback

In this step, organisers refine the current measurement model to reflect the current contest situation. For example, if feedback or new requirements indicate that there are inputs, activities or outputs which need to be incorporated or re-articulated, then refinement suggestions are made to the measurement model.

15.1.3   Phase 3: Learn and Communicate

This phase supports knowledge management on both a specific and general level.

15.1.3.1   Step 1. Analyse

During and after the contest, organisers analyse the contest to record findings, identify problems and make recommendations for best practices.

15.1.3.2   Step 2. Package

The measurement model and the findings are packaged for dissemination, internally among organisers as well as externally in popular and scientific outlets.

15.1.3.3   Step 3. Disseminate

Lessons learned are communicated including the applicability of the measurement model to practice and to research.

15.2   Running Example

We use the example of Travelhack 2013 to illustrate what a measurement model for open digital innovation contests can look like.

15.2.1   Goals

Storstockholms Lokaltrafik (SL) is the public transport company in Stockholm serving 800,000 travellers on a daily basis. Together with Samtrafiken, a company that provides nationwide ticketing and journey planning, SL in September, 2011 launched Trafiklab.se as an open data hub providing public transport data and open platforms to external developers. SL and Samtrafiken, with the support of an independent research institute, designed and organised Travelhack 2013 in the autumn of 2012. This contest had a twofold purpose: (1) to increase the use of the open data platform Trafiklab.se and (2) to stimulate third-party developers to pursue development of novel digital services that make public transport more attractive in the Stockholm region. The main objective was to stimulate distributed open innovation of digital services that enable smart public transport use. This objective was divided into four intended effects of the contest phase:

- five novel digital services, easy to communicate, that enable smart public transport use.
- One hundred and fifty participants (20–30 teams) at the final event.
- Two services that are actively in development and used one year after the contest.
- One service that has reached the top ten in the most downloaded services in the travel category in Sweden three years after the contest (AppStore/Android Market).

15.2.2   Contest Process

Travelhack was based on two fundamental processes: The *Innovation Contest Process* and the *Service Deployment Process*, see Fig. 15.2.

   The *Innovation Contest* process includes three phases: *Planning*, *Ideas* and *Service design*. In the planning phase, the innovation contest is designed and marketed with the goal of attracting participants with profiles that match the goals of the contest organisers. In the ideas phase, the organisers support the participants in generating ideas and select the best ones. In the prototyping phase, organisers

Fig. 15.2 The two
innovation processes of
Travelhack 13 (Ayele et al.
2015, p. 7)

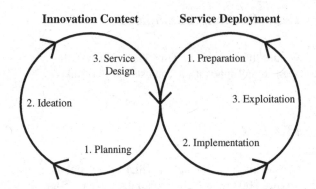

support the participants in developing service prototypes and select winners. In Travelhack 2013, the contest was divided into an ideas phase from which finalists were selected and a service design phase including only finalists that were also given the opportunity to design service prototypes.

The *Service Deployment* process also includes three phases: *Preparation, Implementation* and *Exploitation*. In the preparation phase, the organisers set up goals for service deployment and prepare themselves for meeting these goals. They can choose to be involved at different levels from no involvement at all to full ownership and responsibility for service deployment. In the implementation phase, the service is developed to a commercially viable product and, in the exploitation phase, the service is brought to market. The two processes are interrelated and are connected where selected service prototypes in Phase *3. Service Design* of the Innovation Contest Process moves to Phase *2. Implementation* of the Service Deployment Process.

15.2.3   Measurement Model

The measurement model developed for Travelhack 2013 is described in terms of *Input, Activities, Output* and *Measures*, see Table 15.2. *Input* consists of the resources that the organisers of an innovation contest brings to it. Examples of inputs are open data sources, domain knowledge, time and money. Each phase is divided into *activities* of work that the organisers perform. *Output* is the end result from each of the phases. *Measures* are the measurements used to measure input, activities and output. Measures related to input and activities are viewed as leading indicators, while measures related to output are viewed as lagging indicators.

Table 15.2 The measurement model for the Innovation Contest Process of Travelhack 13 (Ayele et al. 2015, p. 8)

Phase	Planning	Ideas	Service design
Input	Resources, for example, API info., open data sources, domain knowledge, financial resources	Time, resources and facilities	Time, resources and facilities
Activities	a. Specify problem—solution space b. Design contest, i.e., applying the design elements, establish evaluation criteria c. Market contest, i.e., events, website, media coverage, make resources available	a. Support for idea generation, e.g., problem descriptions, personae, meetings, technical support, business model support b. Select finalists: evaluate ideas and business models	a. Support in service design, e.g., hackathon, technical support, business model support b. Select winners: evaluate prototypes and business models
Output	Registered participants ready to contribute to the competition	High quality digital service ideas	High quality digital service prototypes
Measures	• Available resources • Problem—solution maturity • Contest quality • Visibility • Number of participants	• Available resources • Use of available resources • Problem—solution maturity • Quality of support • Time invested by participants • Number of submitted ideas • Ratio of ideas per participant • Number of high quality digital service ideas • Visibility	• Available resources • Use of available resources • Problem—solution maturity • Quality of support • Time invested by participants • Number of digital service prototypes • Ratio of prototypes per participant • Number of high quality digital service prototypes • Visibility

15.2.4 Planning Phase

The organisers of Travelhack 2013 started preparing the contest in the Autumn of 2012. At that time the *problem–solution maturity* could be defined as medium. Two of the contest challenge categories were based on problem areas well understood by the organisers: (1) current users of public transport (PT) lack efficient tools to use effectively PT and (2) non-users of PT lack knowledge about the value of PT. The aim of the last contest category was to increase the problem-solution maturity regarding people with disabilities. Relative to all categories, the solution maturity was low. After the launch in January 2013, the organisers, on a daily basis, monitored the number of participants visiting the contest website as well as the number of teams signing up. They understood that the contest's capability to harness distributed creativity was mirrored through the number of potential participants showing an interest in the contest and they actively used this monitoring to adjust their preparation in terms of marketing efforts. *Visibility* in the media— especially the contest level of penetration through social media—was systematically measured and used as a basis for marketing decisions; e.g., procurement of Facebook marketing. The *contest quality* was at this stage evaluated through the benchmarking of the design, using two focus groups with external developers and prominent members from the open data community. To understand the *quality of support*, the organisers made a structured survey of the participants' support needs later on during the process.

15.2.5 Ideas

The ideas phase was closed on February 5th, 2013. The number of registered teams at this stage was two hundred and thirteen (*number of ideas*) and of these, fifty-four had submitted high quality digital service ideas at a ratio of one idea per team (*ratio of ideas per team* and *number of quality ideas*). This matched the organisers' intent with the three challenge categories. From this set of ideas, a jury using five *defined evaluation criteria* selected twenty-four finalists who were invited to pursue their distributed service design for one month with the aim of transforming their ideas to working prototypes. During this phase, the organisers, through the contest webpage and trafiklab.se, provided team resources such as information about the public transport network, open data and toolboxes to promote end user design (*available resources*). These resources were partly provided based on requests taken from the survey, partly based on the evaluation of the submissions done by the organisers illuminating what the teams needed in order to elevate their ideas to prototypes (*quality of support*). In order to ensure that the final development would take place at the final event, some of the open data resources were only advertised to the teams, but not released until the final. The organisers also continued to measure the *visibility* and impact of the contest in different media channels, for example, by monitoring the contest impact on social media sites and blogs. In order to boost further the visibility of the contest, the organisers made a traditional press release to national and local daily newspapers.

15.2.6 Service Design Phase

Travelhack 2013 ended in March, 2013 with a final 24 h Hackathon. Of the invited finalist teams, twenty-one teams eventually attended. An expert jury, with members from the transport domain, service developers, disability experts and leading members of the open data service community, evaluated and rated the prototypes using a defined set of criteria. The jury members interviewed the teams twice during the final and got pitch presentations from the teams for their judging. During the final, the teams also received on-site and online support from the open data providers advocated by the organisers. The participants were not restricted to use these open data sources, but the open data was selected to provide the teams with suitable sources for their designs. The post contest evaluation indicates that the developers appreciated the organised support, especially that it was available throughout the entire contest. This support design was created based on the survey done prior to the implementation phase. During the contest, one of the APIs malfunctioned, but this issue was resolved within thirty minutes due to the API support standing by. In all, seventy-nine developers in the teams invested one thousand eight hundred and ninety-six hours finalising the twenty-one prototypes during the final event. Each prototype addressed the problem areas on which the contest focused, thereby elevating the organisers' problem–solution maturity from medium to high/very high. The contest also boosted the number of registered users on www.trafiklab.se from seven hundred and fifty to more than two thousand five hundred.

15.2.7   Preparation Phase Running Example

The measurement model for the service deployment process of Travelhack 13 is presented in Table 15.3. To promote the winning prototype transformed into a market ready product, the organisers decided to offer the winning team active support to apply for external development and competence funding (*degree of involvement*) from the National Agency for Innovation in Sweden (Vinnova). The offer was preceded by a joint decision at *top management* level to facilitate a situation wherein the team could re-activate development post contest with the objective of completing the digital prototype ready for market entry within two years of the contest. The degree of support can be defined as option C. Contacts, see Chap. 12. In this case, this meant that the winning team retained the intellectual property of the solution as they developed and performed the majority of the development. The organisers provided complementary support, e.g., to apply for third party funding and provide market information. The winning team accepted the offer from the organisers and transformed itself into a limited company, which enabled the creation of a consortium to apply jointly with the organisers for third party funding in May, 2013.

15.2.8   Implementation Phase Running Example

In the Autumn of 2013, Vinnova awarded the consortium €150,000 to transform the winning prototype into a viable digital service launched on the public within one year from the funding decision. Development work was organised as a project with five inter-related work packages. It began in October, 2013 and ended in January,

Table 15.3 The measurement model for the service deployment process of Travelhack 13 (Ayele et al. 2015, p. 11)

Phase	Preparation	Implementation	Exploitation
Input	Resources, such as open data, knowledge, relationships, time and money	Time and resources depending on the level of post contest support	Time and resources depending on level of post contest support
Activities	a. Decide level of post contest support b. Establish goals for service deployment c. Organise resources based on goals (in a) d. Go/no go decision	a. Support service implementation at various levels (from no support to very high support) b. Evaluate service quality c. Evaluate market potential d. Go/no go decision	a. Support service delivery at various levels (from no support to very high support) b. Support service commercialisation at various levels (from no support to very high support) c. Continual evaluation of service quality and market potential
Output	Prepared organisation	Viable digital service, business model and intellectual property	Service revenue
Measures	• Level of post-contest support • Available resources • Level of commitment	• Available resources • Quality of support • Problem—solution maturity • Service demand	• Available resources • Quality of support • Problem—solution maturity • Service use • Rate of diffusion • Number of downloads • Revenues

2015. During that time the organisers provided *available resources* to the development effort in different ways within the support scope defined. *Service demand* was measured through the involvement of end users throughout the design phase and by user test panels during the pilot test phase. These evaluation efforts provided input to increase the organisers' *problem-solution maturity* regarding knowledge about how travellers with cognitive disorders use PT. By an in-depth evaluation of the process, the organisers also increased their knowledge about post contest service implementation, which increased their problem-solution maturity regarding distributed digital innovation based on open resources.

15.2.9   Exploitation Phase Running Example

In September, 2014, the winning team, now operating as a limited company, entered the public market by releasing the first version of Resledaren on Android

Store and iOS app. store. As the organisers had decided to limit their level of support to the implementation phase, this case does not cover the exploitation phase described in the measurement model.

15.3 Guidelines

Formal evaluation of open digital innovation contests provides important information for the organisers. The information is used to manage the contest and its aftermath, service deployment. Moreover, the information is used to support learning, both internally among organisers and externally as part of the scientific knowledge base.

- Design a measurement model specific to the needs of a particular open digital innovation contest.
- Re-use knowledge from previous open digital innovation contests when designing a new measurement model.
- Limit the measurement model to ensure relevance and ease of use.

15.4 Further Reading

This chapter is primarily based on two references: Ayele et al. (2015, 2016). Ayele et al. (2015) present the digital innovation contest measurement model for Travelhack 2013 and in Ayele (2016), the method for designing measurement models for digital innovation contests are presented. The two papers add depth to how the model and the method were designed as well as the literature and the empirical evaluations on which they were based.

References

Ayele, W., Juell-Skielse, G., Hjalmarsson, A., Johannesson, P., & Rudmark, D. (2015). Evaluating open data innovation: A measurement model for digital innovation contests. *Proceedings of Pacific Asia conference on information systems (PACIS).* Singapore.

Ayele, W., Hjalmarsson, A., Juell-Skielse, G., & Johannesson, P. (2016). *A method for designing and evaluating digital innovation contest and service deployment evaluation models.* Pre-ICIS Workshop "Practice-based Design and Innovation of Digital Artifacts", Association of Information Systems.

Hansen, M. T., & Birkinshaw, J. (2007). The innovation value chain. *Harvard Business Review,* 85(6), 121–130.

Appendix
Rules for the Open Digital Innovation Contest "Olympic City Transport Challenge"

Introduction

The Olympic City Transport Challenge is designed to encourage all interested parties (each a "Contestant") to use their creativity to develop new innovative digital services, helping citizens and visitors to transport themselves around Rio, both during the Rio Olympic Games and beyond. Viktoria Swedish ICT ("Viktoria") is responsible for and arranges the Contest. The City of Rio de Janeiro will actively participate and promote the winning service under the brand Cidade Olímpica[1] that the winner will use after the Contest. Evry AB ("Evry") will provide the technology and support of the developers' platform.

Who Can Participate?

Any company, individual or team of individuals is welcome to participate in the Olympic City Transport Challenge. However, companies or individuals with ties to the jury members are not eligible to participate.

Important Dates

The Contest is divided into several stages, encompassing a number of milestones and related activities. The Contest Period begins on November 1, 2015 and is scheduled as follows:

2015-11-03 Registration opens
2015-12-07 Concept submission

---

[1]http://www.cidadeolimpica.com.br/en/

© Springer International Publishing AG 2017
A. Hjalmarsson et al., *Open Digital Innovation*, Progress in IS,
DOI 10.1007/978-3-319-56339-8

2015-12-21 Announcement of finalists
2016-03-15 Application Submission, including non-mandatory links to published apps
2016-04-01 Finale and Categories Winners are appointed.

Submission Requirements

The aim of the Contest is to facilitate development of smartphone apps helping citizens and visitors at the Olympic Games in Rio de Janeiro 2016. All submissions are done through the contest website.

Overall Requirements

All contestants will be granted access to the developers' platform. Information on how to obtain access to the platform can be retrieved from the contest website.

The winning app should be able to support two languages (English and Portuguese). The language in the submitted app should therefore either be English or Portuguese, or both English and Portuguese.

The contest includes two submissions, one for the concept phase and one for the implementation phase.

Concept Phase Submission

The concept phase submission should include an idea description and be submitted through the contest website. The idea description could consist of text, pictures or other media and must include:

Description of the app
User benefits—how the app addresses the challenge
Feasibility and potential stoppers
A selected number of participants will be invited to continue into the implementation phase.

Implementation Phase Submission

The implementation phase submission must include an description of the service and may also include, if applicable, information about the published app in an application marketplace or a link to a web site. The submissions in done through Contest website.

The app description could consist of text, pictures or other media and must include:

- Description of the app
- User benefits—how the app addresses the challenge.

If the submission is a smartphone app the submission could include a link to the published app in or more of the following application marketplaces:

- Apple Appstore
- Google Play
- Windows Marketplace.

If the submission is a web application the submission could include a link to the web site.

Since it is crucial that the service is launched prior to the Olympics, contestants that have not published their service by March 15 need to include convincing arguments that the service will be ready before June 1st.

Evaluation Criteria

The evaluation of the Implementation Phase Submissions will be done in two steps.

1. First, the Jury (appointed by Viktoria) will assess which of the concept phase submissions that are qualified to meet the challenge of the contest. No more than 50 submissions will go through to the implementation phase.
2. Second, a winner will be appointed based on criteria related to (a) the degree which the app meets the challenge (b) usability (c) contestants ability to finalize and sustain the service (d) innovative use of open data.

These assessments are final and cannot be appealed.

Prizes

The prize for the winning team is the usage of the Cidade Olímpica brand, controlled by the Rio de Janeiro City Hall. The use of the brand will effectively support the winning teams in attaining fast recognition for their services.

Moreover, the winning teams of challenge category 2. Comfort and accessibility and 3. Experiencing the Olympic Games will also receive 25.000 SEK for travelling to Rio de Janeiro prior to the Olympic Games.

Since services launched under the Cidade Olímpica brand will be available after the Olympic Games, we would like to put attention to contestants that some maintenance may be needed by contestants also after the Olympic Games. The objective of the contest is to promote services that improve transportation on a long-term basis.

Intellectual Property

The Contestant(s) retains ownership of all intellectual property rights in and to its intellectual property used and/or incorporated in the developed App, including documentation, submitted to the Challenge. However, the organizers of the contest maintain the right to use Submissions for communicative purposes.

Index

© Springer International Publishing AG 2017
A. Hjalmarsson et al., *Open Digital Innovation*, Progress in IS,
DOI 10.1007/978-3-319-56339-8

Printed in the United States
By Bookmasters